Cambridge Elements

Elements in Twenty-First Century Music Practice
edited by
Simon Zagorski-Thomas
London College of Music, University of West London

HIDDEN MUSIC

The Composer's Guide to Sonification

Milton Mermikides
University of Surrey

Shaftesbury Road, Cambridge CB2 8EA, United Kingdom

One Liberty Plaza, 20th Floor, New York, NY 10006, USA

477 Williamstown Road, Port Melbourne, VIC 3207, Australia

314–321, 3rd Floor, Plot 3, Splendor Forum, Jasola District Centre, New Delhi – 110025, India

103 Penang Road, #05–06/07, Visioncrest Commercial, Singapore 238467

Cambridge University Press is part of Cambridge University Press & Assessment, a department of the University of Cambridge.

We share the University's mission to contribute to society through the pursuit of education, learning and research at the highest international levels of excellence.

www.cambridge.org
Information on this title: www.cambridge.org/9781009500319

DOI: 10.1017/9781009258555

© Milton Mermikides 2025

This publication is in copyright. Subject to statutory exception and to the provisions of relevant collective licensing agreements, no reproduction of any part may take place without the written permission of Cambridge University Press & Assessment.

When citing this work, please include a reference to the DOI 10.1017/9781009258555

First published 2025

A catalogue record for this publication is available from the British Library

ISBN 978-1-009-50031-9 Hardback
ISBN 978-1-009-25857-9 Paperback
ISSN 2633-4585 (online)
ISSN 2633-4577 (print)

Additional resources for this publication at www.cambridge.org/Mermikides

Cambridge University Press & Assessment has no responsibility for the persistence or accuracy of URLs for external or third-party internet websites referred to in this publication and does not guarantee that any content on such websites is, or will remain, accurate or appropriate.

Hidden Music

The Composer's Guide to Sonification

Elements in Twenty-First Century Music Practice

DOI: 10.1017/9781009258555
First published online: January 2025

Milton Mermikides
University of Surrey
Author for correspondence: Milton Mermikides, miltonline@me.com

Abstract: This Element explores the intersection of data sonification (the systematic translation of data into sound) and musical composition. Section 1 engages with existing discourse and offers an original model (the *sonification continuum*) which provides perspectives on the practice of sonification for composers, science communicators and those interested in this rapidly emerging field. Section 2 engages with the sonification process itself, exploring techniques, models of translation, data fidelity, analogic and symbolic data mapping, temporality and the listener experience. In Section 3 these concepts and techniques are all made concrete in the context of a selection of the author's projects (2004–2023). Finally, some reasons are offered on how sonification as a practice might enrich composition, communication, collaboration and a sense of connection.

This Element also has a video abstract: www.cambridge.org/EMUP_Mermikides_abstract

Keywords: sonification, data, music, composition, parameter mapping

© Milton Mermikides 2025

ISBNs: 9781009500319 (HB), 9781009258579 (PB), 9781009258555 (OC)
ISSNs: 2633-4585 (online), 2633-4577 (print)

Contents

1 The Sonification Continuum   1

2 The Sonification Process   19

3 The Sonification Experience   43

    References   67

Note to Reader: the text of this entire Element has been sonified, and is offered as a gentle optional background accompaniment to the reading experience.

1 The Sonification Continuum

Music is continuous, it is only listening that is intermittent.

John Cage[1]

1.1 Prelude: Background

The craft of collecting objective, measurable facts and information ('data') and constructing systematic processes to represent them in sound ('sonification') has been a central part of my compositional practice for over twenty years. This approach has produced hundreds of audio and multimedia outputs, collaborative projects, presentations, masterclasses, broadcasts and events with a wide range of scientists and institutions. Despite this level of engagement, it has never been an approach I was introduced to formally or guided through. However, when looking back it appears to have evolved along an unplanned path guided by landmarks and faint signposts. Some of these were moments of diverting curiosity and others almost overwhelming personal experiences that somehow called me to engage with sonification, but with rigour, honesty and sincerity. These experiences were essentially my teachers in the craft and include the following:

(a) An early life at CERN (Geneva, Switzerland), where scientific curiosity and a fresh and total musical immersion were unified by a shared sense of discovery and wonder.
(b) An exhibit at CERN, where passing photons which happened to drift and end their light-years of travel in the vicinity emitted a click in a satisfying and mesmeric ungridded rhythm.
(c) Childhood summers in Greece, staring at the night sky and transcribing a melodic contour in the stars.
(d) The discovery of computer music, the MIDI and DAW environments, and generative music where a nexus of simple objective instructions led to a richness of subjective musical experience.
(e) Encountering the practice of musical cryptogram in the BACH and Shostakovich motifs, alongside the *milimetrazação* (graphing or millimetrisation)[2] technique of Villa-Lobos's *New York Skyline Melody* – whose melody (and architecture) I know as well as any conventionally conceived melodic contour.[3]

---

[1] John Cage cited in Millar and Cage, 2010:74.
[2] See Enyart,1984:188 and Slonimsky, 1945:6.
[3] For a visualization we produced of Villa-Lobos's *New York Skyline Melody,* see Tanczos (2014).

(f) First hearing the sonified output of my engagement with Rilke's thought experiment (see Section 3.1.1 Primal Sound) – a piece of music (which has had a life beyond its origin) that I neither had expected from the process nor could otherwise imagine.

(g) Sonifying my daily blood results from my hospital bed while undergoing treatment for leukaemia (see Section 3.1.2 Bloodlines).

(h) Experiencing a reaction to a medication which caused the pitch Bb2 to create an intense frisson experience. The effect was so pronounced and repeatable that, despite not having perfect pitch, I could – using the 'chill level' as an analytical tool – transcribe chords and melodies.

(i) Using our yet-to-be daughter's embryo scan to generate a piece of music[4] – an ode using objectively sourced pitch and rhythmic data despite the uncertainty of her future existence.

(j) The cascade of data-musical insights, revelations from the Sound Asleep project (Section 3.1.5).

(k) Deciding on the morning of a TEDx presentation to translate the audience selecting their seating positions into sound, conceiving and enacting the system and presenting it to them at the end of my talk (Section 3.1.8).

(l) Running a digital image of Monet's *Water Lilies* through my newly created Kandinsky patch – a piece of coding that translates colour data into discrete and continuous pitch material (see Section 3.1.9).

Experiences such as these are rich and integrate my musical and personal life. And somehow, when I belatedly arrived at the academic literature – as thoughtful and useful as it is – it did not resonate fully with my experiences and fundamental motivations. The perspectives I encountered tended to present either somewhat prescriptive and proscriptive definitions of data sonification, or 'anything goes' compositional tools where data is selected, reworked, manipulated and even abandoned in service of a musical end. In the domain of 'pure' data sonification, music is treated with suspicion as a potential distortion of data communication, where composers cannot be trusted to resist aesthetic urges rather than staying 'true to the data'. This wariness towards musical intent in the context of data sonification is apparent even in key academic music texts: *The Oxford Handbook of Computer Music* has a chapter on data sonification but 'data music' (Worrall, 2011) is addressed only in a final subsection, where it exists on a 'continuum' of sonification engagement. More tellingly, the chapter on data sonification in *The Oxford Handbook of Algorithmic Music* is entitled 'Sonification ≠ Music' (Scaletti, 2021), laying bare the supposed distinction. Such positions contain valid

---
[4] *Two Blue Circles for Classical Guitar and Electronics* (Mermikides, 2020b).

underlying concerns, particularly Neuhoff's (2019) clear identification of the challenges and potential limits of sonification. I too favour clear, unfudged data – and scientific – communication, and I strongly advocate prioritising data communication over 'sonic entertainment' to overcome barriers of literacy, numeracy and visualisation (see Sawe et al., 2020) and to enhance physical development and rehabilitation (see for example, Scholz et al., 2016). And yet to separate data communication from musical mechanics appears to me to make an unhelpful opposition, for as I shall discuss later, it rests on assumptions on the definition and limits of 'music'. I have since found some kinship in the sonification works of John Luther Adams, Xenakis, Cage and members of the International Community for Auditory Display (ICAD), but equally, I have recognised traces of sonification in many 'conventional' works, and these traces have proved just as stimulating.

There are others who allow scientific and artistic sonification to have hybrid goals, as in Gresham-Lancaster's warning that 'science must be inclusive of craftsmanship and artistry, and vice versa, for this field to be fully accepted and realise the usefulness and promise of these important tools' (Gresham-Lancaster, 2012:212). Nonetheless, the distinction between data sonification and a loose form of data music (where the data is often seen as inspirational 'source' material rather than central to the music itself) still persists as in Neuhoff's 'bifurcation' of 'empirical' and 'artistic sonification' and his characterisation of any hybrid goals as a 'muddled middle' (Neuhoff, 2019). This wariness of the middle ground between the artistic and empirical aims of sonification may be well motivated, but it rests on narrow definitions of both music and communication of information, compromising two immediate scientific and artistic opportunities. Firstly, data communication can and should exploit the wealth of compositional tools and strategies available. Secondly, the challenge of representing data fairly tests and extends a composer's skills and potential outputs; it exposes hidden preconceptions about music while revealing its deep possibilities. If we accept music itself as a form of sonic communication – that is, the expression in sound of such information as patterns, processes, thoughts, narrative structures and states of emotion, mind or place, where sound includes speech, natural sounds, sound design, noise and pitch – then it becomes less clear, less useful to draw a hard line between data sonification and music.

Thus, I have never thought of data sonification (and/or data music)[5] as the novel and fleeting diversion from conventional music-making that it appears to

---

[5] Definitions and delineations of data sonification, data music, sonification and other terms are addressed directly in Section 1.2.

be with others, but as a fundamental part of my musical purpose. My approach often contests the boundaries between data sonification and broadly defined composition. When I have felt a composition to be successful, it has been because the data and its inherent patterns did more than provide a creative constraint or tribute; rather, they *mattered* in terms of sonic output, genuinely dictating and informing fundamental aspects of the compositional process and the experience of the listener where the data and its inherent patterns not only provide a creative constraint and tribute to the work, but *matter* in terms of sonic output. In collating and exhibiting some of my works in 2007, I hurriedly coined the moniker *Hidden Music*. This phrase, which implies that there is a music *inherent* in the data waiting to be unearthed, rather than music made from reshaping 'data material', has proved reliably and increasingly apt, and so I have retained it as a title for this Element. In these pages, I aim to illuminate the intersection of sonification and compositional practice, and to complement the existing literature for practitioners, science communicators and those interested in this young and promising field. In fact, the deeper my exploration of this craft, the more convinced I become that there is a complementary relationship between conventional musical theory – *the nature of music* – and data sonification – *the music of nature*. The former involves identifying and manipulating objective data in music, while the latter involves the sonic representation of objective data. In either domain, analytical models, concepts and technologies may be routinely flipped in order to pass material from one to the other – from data to music or music to data.

Despite the academic context of this Element, it aims to explore – rather than dictate – relevant ideas and approaches in a manner accessible and practical to composers, theorists and others. A history and/or survey of contemporary sonification practice is beyond the scope of this Element, particularly given problems of definition and boundaries.[6] Instead, I present conceptual and practical ideas to help the reader chart their own course, with selections of my work serving as examples (and not exemplars) of the underlying themes. Section 1 is concerned with first principles, addressing the complex of definitions, challenges and opportunities – essentially, the *what* of sonification. Section 2 confronts the *how* of sonification: principles, strategies, techniques and technologies of translations from the data to the sonic realm. Section 3 presents a selection of my works from the past two decades in order to illustrate these approaches in action, followed by some thoughts on the – or at least my – *why* of sonification.

---

[6] For an excellent introduction and overview of empirical sonification practice, see Supper (2016).

1.2 Unweaving Definitions

This Element is concerned with the set of practices that involve the communication of data through sound (including music). Depending on one's definition of data and communication, questions of boundary arise with the representation of any extra-musical content in music – be it the sophisticated language of talking drums in sub-Saharan Africa (Gleick, 2011:18–23), the sonic lightning bolts in Beethoven's Sixth Symphony, Joni Mitchell's ad hoc guitar tunings to 'the crows and the seagulls, and sonic references available' (Mitchell, 1994: 0:32–38), Villa-Lobos's use of the *Belo Horizonte* mountain skyline as thematic material in Symphony no. 6 (Enyart, 1984:188), Aphex Twin's embedding of images in the spectrographs of electronic works (see Buckle, 2022), the Tuvan *borbannadir* throat singing technique of closely imitating bubbling brooks (Aksenov, 1973) or any other innumerable examples. Even with more constrained definitions, there are numerous terms for the craft including sonification, data sonification ('datason'), audification, musical translation, auditory display, musification, data music, and data-, data-driven or data-based composition. This proliferation of variously defined and overlapping terms emerges not just from the rapid and unfettered evolution of this type of practice in an increasingly 'datarised' world, but from questions of intents, motivations, adherence to various systems of data selection and collection, and the ultimate use and reception. Some commenters have attempted to strictly define and demarcate these terms, most particularly in the delineation of a strictly defined data sonification (or simply 'sonification') from other artistic practices (see, for example, Hermann, 2010; Barrass & Vickers, 2011; Neuhoff, 2019; and Scaletti, 2021).

A commonly referenced description in the literature is 'the use of non-speech audio to convey information' (Kramer et al., 1999:1). Other definitions share a similar basic structure: a communication of information in sound, but with a caveat, the exception of the 'normal' sonic communication of speech, a 'seeing with our ears' (Vickers, 2016: 135). While some definitions focus on a systematic and reproducible *process*, others add a condition of the *purpose* of the process, such as a "mapping of numerically represented relations in some realm under study" to relations in an acoustic realm *for the purpose of interpreting, understanding, or communicating relations in the domain under study*" (italics added) (quoted in Barrass & Vickers, 2011:147) or Worrall's 'acoustic representation of data for relational interpretation by listeners, *for the purpose* of increasing their knowledge of the source from which the data was acquired' (Worrall, 2009: 314 – italics added). So while some sort of translation of data into sound is a basic requirement, the type (and method of collection) of data, translation process, level of intervention or faithfulness and the purpose of the sonification, provide for various commenters additional criteria to this core requirement.

Though my work in this field happens to align with a more faithful and systematic representation of data than many of my sonification-curious colleagues, I find Baxter's perspective of treating sonification 'more of a verb rather than a noun, a technique to be used, rather than a thing to be arrived at' (Baxter, 2020:16) to be a helpful parry to the challenges of precise definition. Nonetheless, it is illuminating and helpful to interrogate our definitions of (data) sonification, and any hidden presumptions, inconsistencies and implications involved, which we now explore.

1.3 The Boundaries of Sonification and the Music of Music

Rather than rely dutifully on pre-existing definitions, I invite the reader to develop their own understanding and categorisations of the field. As a necessary (but not perhaps sufficient) condition for discussion, let us agree that all sonification entails a translation of some information into sound. The encoding of information and its transmission to a recipient invites engagement with Shannon's information theory, entropy and cryptography.[7] How the information is transmitted, the 'key' to its encoding, the degree to which its entropy (or conversely, its level of order) is preserved amidst 'noise', and whether the received signal can be decoded to reveal the original message, is a simple but clear framing of the challenge and craft of data sonification. Incidentally, this description applies to music in general, if one accepts that information includes the meaningful brain activity of emotional states (see Stark, Vuust & Kringelbach, 2018). If we understand *meaningful* in its usual senses of valuable, recognisable and not directly expressible, and if we take the *sender* and *receiver* to refer to human brains and *sound* as the transmission channel through which the signal is sent, then we arrive at a description of musical communication I am happy to accept.

So far, then, we have said that data sonification involves a transfer of information – meaningful signals – from sender to receiver, via some form of encoding. Unlike in conventional music, these meaningful signals do not necessarily originate from musical ideas or a complex of patterns in human brains, but from external data. We might picture the sonification process as a membrane through which data (observed properties in the domain under study) pass through to become sound, or 'readily sounded' material such as captured audio or musical instructions. This membrane divides the *data realm*

---

[7] See, for example, Shannon, 1948: 379–423, 623–656 and Gleick 2011: 191–217.

(observed information) from the *sonic realm* (sounding or readily sounded objects), even as it provides access to both.

What constitutes material in the data realm? An essential definition may be 'observed facts and information'; however, the process of collection (scientifically objective or otherwise) and intended use (e.g. information collected for reference or analysis, etc.) of the data may differ between individuals, as in Scaletti's 'purposes' earlier. What does seem to be fundamental for data sonification (and sonification more broadly) is that there is a significant degree of objectivity in the data set; the data is collected (or to some degree selected) rather than created specifically for the purpose of sonification. If the data is mined, manipulated or ignored freely, then the process becomes closer to conventional composition, albeit through an elaborate pantomime: the system is played by a human like an instrument, rather than having the sonic output dictated by the observed material. All may be fair in composition, some ends may justify some means, and the piece may not exist at all without the original impetus. And yet such a process, I argue, cannot be called sonification. Even with artistic or loose approaches, sonification entails a delegation of decisions to the data: no matter how intricate the hands-on system design, there is a significant hands-off moment, where the system is allowed to run free of intervention. How this delegation might be assessed, and the extent to which it reaches stricter definitions of data sonification, are explored further in Sections 1.4 and 2.1.

So the manner of data collection might affect one's assessment of what type of sonification a process is – or whether it is sonification at all. But what of the data itself? Is any type of data – if collected objectively – allowable? Suppose we set up a technological device to somehow sample rapidly (over 40,000 times a second, say) changing air pressure, convert and store this information to a series of discrete values and then later reverse the process, using the captured data to recreate similar changes in air pressure. Is this sonification? This is, of course, a mischievous description of digital audio recording which – despite being a very clear example of objectively collected data being sounded – is excluded from conventional definitions of data sonification. Is a flute performance a sonification of the flautist's manipulation of air pressure and finger movements – to say nothing of the musical symbols on the page or the composer's abstracted ideas? There is no end to such Socratically awkward examples: imagine placing a sensor under each key of a piano keyboard which measures when, how long and how fast (or hard) each key is pressed, and this data is stored numerically and then used to replay digital audio samples of a piano at analogous pitch frequencies, durations and velocities. Is this a sonification of the keyboardist's performance, even if we systematically manipulate the data (via transposition, scaling the velocity, doubling at octaves or triggering alternate instruments)? These descriptions of digital audio, a flautist's performance and a MIDI instrument are all clear examples of 'objective data' being 'mapped to sound' in a way that can 'convey information' of the 'domain under study' (all descriptions found in Section 1.2). Why then would these *not* be defined as sonification (data or otherwise) or data music? And why, for that matter, is speech – perhaps the clearest example of information being imparted through sound – explicitly excluded from many definitions of sonification? One possible response has been suggested, namely, that when data is generated to produce a particular sound, the resulting sound cannot be considered a sonification. We should be careful with this line of reasoning, however, for we will later see examples of how musical data can be sonified. Another possible response is that they are indeed examples of sonifications, but so established, conventional or mundane that they seem fundamentally different from the more novel auditory displays.[8] But our model of data and sonic realms offers an explanation that I prefer: that digital audio, musical notation, MIDI information and so on – although they are expressible as data – can be thought to already lie in the sonic realm in our model (which includes sound or material that is readily sounded). Turning this 'sonic data' into sound is, I suggest, usually a manipulation (recording, performance, editing, sequencing, transcription) *within* the sonic realm rather than a cross-realm translation through the sonification boundary. What seemed a simple description of data sonification (data translated into sound) becomes a rather puzzling recursive cycle of questions. We might also suggest why, for example, speech – and implicitly audio, notational and other 'sonic' forms of information – is explicitly excluded from common descriptions of sonification: speech is an established sonification practice, while the others already inhabit the sonic realm.

Figure 1 illustrates a number of these relationships. A sonification membrane separates the data and sonic realms. But this boundary is porous: material can travel from the data to the sonic realm using various techniques(see Section 2.3).

The sonic realm might be further subdivided into four domains:

1. The *audio domain*, which includes stored or transitory analogue and digital audio material.
2. The *instrumental domain*, which includes acoustic and electronic instruments, sequencers and their human and machine performers.

---

[8] Scaletti (2021) attests that music is in fact a sonification – of musical thought, a concept that is discussed later. Readers unfamiliar with this field's terms of art might be struck by the novel use of *display* to refer to something heard rather than seen; but to display – etymologically, 'to unfurl' – data in sound is surely an apt metaphor for the sonification process.

3. The (musical) *symbol domain*, which consists of symbolic representations and instructions, notations (from conventional to graphic), MIDI, timelines and other abstracted scripts and instructions (whether written, stored or not).
4. The *acoustic domain*, that is, patterns of air pressure within the audio spectrum and the listeners' auditory faculties and perceptions.

The data realm is loosely subdivided into data that is empirical (directly observed) or abstracted (simulated and analysed). To illustrate the distinction, consider a bouncing ball: we can obtain empirical data by directly observing the ball as it bounces; abstract data, on the other hand, is yielded by an algorithm that outputs the vertical position of a virtual sphere based on the elasticity of the object and the surface together with gravitational laws.[9]

Of course, material can be manipulated *within* domains. Examples are not far to seek: in the audio domain, sound can be converted from analogue to digital; in the music symbol domain, a MIDI file can be translated into staff notation; in the instrumental domain, a work can be arranged for a different instrument or ensemble. Material can also be translated *between* two domains – for example, sampling and recording (acoustic to audio), transcription (acoustic to music), playback (audio to acoustic) and so on. Certainly, the focus of this Element is the inter-realm sonification boundary and the challenge of transmitting information across it, yet 'inter-domain' boundaries are hardly perfect information-preserving channels either. Consider Alvin Lucier's *Sitting in a Room*: a passage of speech is repeatedly played back and recorded in a room (it is neatest if the passage consists of the instructions for and concept behind the piece). The resulting disintegration – intelligible speech dissolving gradually into throbbing rhythm amid the room's resonance – beautifully demonstrates the information loss (or transformation) at the audio-acoustic boundary (see 'Lucier's loop' in Figure 1).[10] Ultimately the signal represents the rhythm – but not the spoken message – of the voice, together with the acoustic characteristics of the room and recording technology. I propose other loops and tests of boundaries, such as a repeated audio-to-MIDI-bounce loop, or – more critically to musical

---

[9] See, for example, Dillon Bastan's aptly titled *Inspired by Nature* suite of plugins which generate in real-time MIDI and audio material based on editable gravitational, swarming and other naturally derived algorithms (Bastan, 2022).

[10] In this type of inter-domain loop we can also place other disintegration pieces in which sonic material is repeatedly sent through a tape recording process, deteriorating the original signal (see Basinksi's *Disintegration Loops*). *Mémoires/Erosion*, by Tristan Murail, adopts such an idea, but here live material from the soloist is repeatedly 'reinjected' into a live ensemble, which emulates a tape machine, distorting the solo material through the instrumental domain until 'the tuning goes away, the rhythmic contours are massaged, the timbres drift into non-harmonic sound and what began as a simple repeated figure has been transformed into a dense, chaotic texture' (Anderson, 1997).

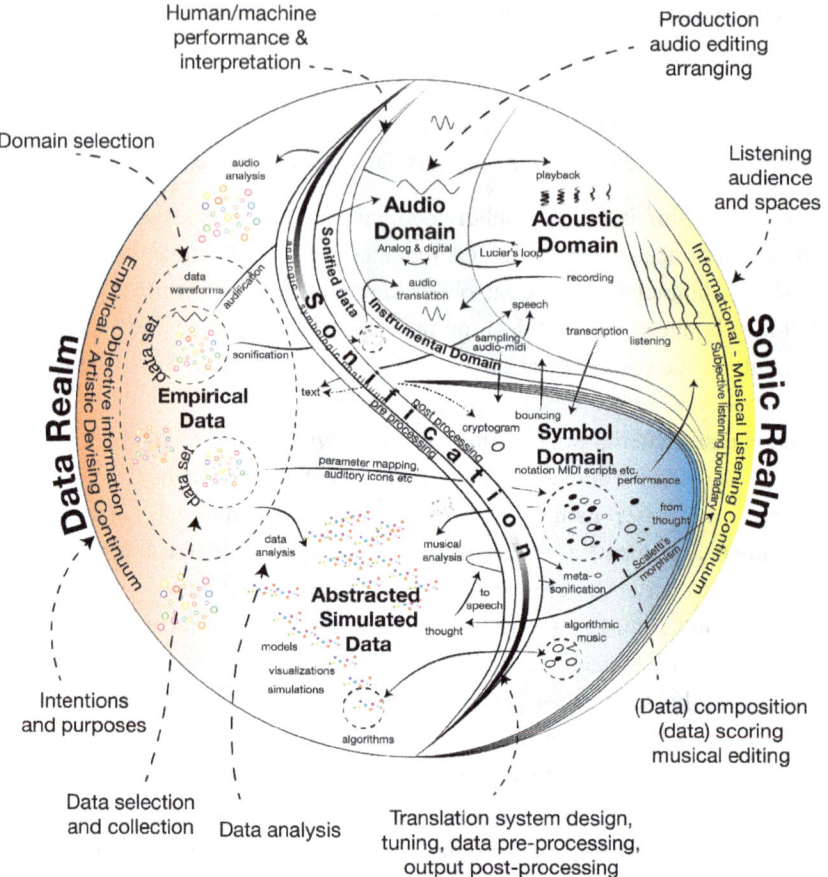

Figure 1 An illustration of the 'Sonification continuum', where the data and sonic realms (and their various domains) are separated by the sonification boundary. Some sonification practices and themes are indicated between domains and realms. Points of human input – the 'composer's hand' – from outside the model are shown with dashed arrows.

practice – an assessment of what pertinent rhythmic, pitch and timbral information is lost at the acoustic–notation boundary (see Wishart & Emmerson, 1996:26, and Mermikides, 2010:82–167).

While one key boundary for discussion is that between the data and sonic realms, there exists another boundary that is just as crucial: that between the sonic realm and the listener — the *subjective listening boundary*. We can construct an elegant translation system which packs relevant information into a sonic signal, but it may be completely unrecognisable to all listeners, even the composer. The ultimate criteria for a successful sonification may vary according to its maker. For one sonifier,[11] it may be crucial that the data set can be derived from the sonification precisely and efficiently, regardless of any other listening experience. For another sonifier, it may matter less that the listener can identify the particular mappings, but that they feel (hear musically) changes in the data domain. Still another sonifier might employ data translation entirely freely or partially, or as an impetus, a hidden 'Easter egg' or creative exercise, and choose not to reveal everything – or anything – about the process to the listener.

Figure 1 takes a similar broad view to Shannon's (1948) model and other representations of information flow and encoding, as well as familiar depictions of sonification processes, such as Grond and Berger's 'map for a general design process of parameter mapping sonification' (Grond & Berger, 2011:366). In their model a data domain (again on the left) of 'rigorous objectivity' is integrated through 'conscious intervention' to a signal domain (on the right) which involves a 'subjective component'. But Figure 1 incorporates other existing – and some novel – perspectives on sonification practices and theories. These include Neuhoff's bifurcation of empirical and artistic sonification, which I have illustrated as the 'empirical-artistic devising continuum' on the left side of the model. This permits the possibility of hybrid sonification goals and also allows for a decoupling of a project's intended purpose from its ultimate use and reception, explored in Section 1.4. The listener's reception of the sonification – with an acknowledgement of Grond and Berger's 'subjective component' – is represented on the right hand of the diagram as the 'informational-musical listening continuum': this again allows the possibility that a sonification can meet two goals – conveying information, including Barrass and Vickers's 'everyday' and 'diagnostic' listening, and giving musical satisfaction, even if at times this 'duality of music and sonification' is 'constraining, or even inherently conflicting' (Barrass & Vickers, 2011). In Section 3.2 I reject the notion that because musical listening is transporting (occasionally or inherently), it cannot therefore be informative. In fact, trained musicians, when listening to music, do not fall into some kind of aesthetic trance: they habitually analyse the mechanics behind musical communication – the reasons behind the musical impact, however instinctive and immediate it is. Furthermore, I suggest (as many have since Russollo and Cage)[12] that it's possible to listen to the most quotidian of sounds with a musical ear: take the cross-rhythm of the indicator clicks and windscreen wipers, the pitch interval within and between car horns, and the implied metre of tyres moving over road markings. It's also perfectly possible to fully hear and appreciate the musical mechanics and underlying

---

[11] Let us use the term 'sonifier' as someone carrying out a sonification process (see Baxter, 2020:9).
[12] See Holmes (2020).

construction of a piece of music without falling into ecstatic oblivion. In short, listening can be both musical and informational – and to musicians it is often both.

The sonification membrane (the S shape in the centre of Figure 1) is not just a one-way valve translating data to sonic material; it also allows the collection of objective data from the sonic realm, as with musical and audio analysis. Under this model, the sonic material data might itself be sonified, passing through the sonification membrane again. Even while manipulating sonic data is seen here as activity within the sonic realm, it is possible to draw data from musical, acoustic and other sonic material, and convey that information sonically, allowing us to reveal novel information about the original sonic material. We could, for example, take Björk's corpus and derive from it song structures, with short sonic markers identifying similar sections (verses, chorus, bridges, etc.), combining them to form structural representations at a fraction of the original durations. This might reveal in a moment the artist's evolving and comparative diversification from standard templates. We might also present the relative frequency of pitch classes in a Bach fugue (or Bach's entire musical corpus transposed to one key) and use this data to play the 12 pitch classes in order of frequency (as in number of occurrences); alternatively, their relative frequencies could be linked to durations or velocities, or indeed a wholly different but still musical representation of this data.

Such sonifications as these do not represent the source material itself but data *about* it, convincingly meeting Scaletti's criteria of 'interpreting, understanding, or communicating relations in the domain under study'. These transformations of sonic material ('recursive' or 'meta-sonifications', indicated as a loop in Figure 1) can meet either of Neuhoff's (2019) subcategories of empirical and artistic sonification, but despite his recommendation to 'avoid the muddled middle', I see no reason why they cannot satisfy both goals completely. Take, for example, the track(s) *Every Recording of Gymnopedie 1* (Hey Exit, 2015), where a large (but unspecified number) of superimposed recordings of Satie's *Gymnopédie* no. 1 are time-stretched to the duration of the longest recording. The resulting heterophonic landscape of variously coordinated and disparate performances presents – objectively – tacitly agreed passages of relative rigidity and flexibility. It also – for me – operates entirely as a piece of music where the original piece is present (many times over) but another crystalline, systematically ambient piece emerges where non-diatonic harmonic shifts are variously blurred and exaggerated. I use similar superimpositions in research and teaching – for example by overlaying an original written melody of Pat Martino's over his performed interpretations (Mermikides, 2010:154–167). The resulting conversation between the melodic template and fluid and (often tantalisingly) delayed improvisatory performance reveals more of his individualistic melodic voice than in the original performance: A music of the music.

The *sonification continuum* in Figure 1 does not attempt to prescribe definitions, but to illuminate the various interweaving domains, continua and opportunities for practice. We can recognize any individual's definition of (data) sonification, strict or loose as it may be, as a particular set of pathways from data to sound. It also indicates – with dashed arrows – some regions where human intervention in the processes might occur: these include proposing the project and defining its purpose, selecting the field of study and its data, designing the translation process, and producing and presenting its sonic output; the act of listening, too, is a human intervention. These various interventions effect, affect, fine-tune and frame a 'true' translation process, or, for artistic purposes, might contextualise and manipulate the sonification process with 'the composer's hand' (Baxter 2020:9). The extent to which these are compatible, and how we might ascertain a sense of data 'truthfulness' are explored in Sections 1.5 and 2.1.

1.4 Where the Wind Blows: Abstractions and Purposes

In order to test the picture of sonification given earlier, let's consider a particular project with a series of progressive alterations, with some non-rhetorical but possibly irritating questions on the extent to which they meet the criteria of data sonification (if at all). By way of reminder, some representative definitions from Section 1.2 include the following:

- 'the use of non-speech sound to convey information, typically through the mapping of data and data relations to properties of an acoustic signal'
- 'the auditory equivalent of scientific visualization'
- 'a mapping of numerically represented relations in some domain under study to relations in an acoustic realm for the purpose of interpreting, understanding, or communicating relations in the realm under study'.

Now let us begin our thought experiment and compare the following three scenarios:

(a) The leaves on a tree at a particular location (say on the Peloponnese coast) rustling in the changing wind.
(b) A wind chime is set up in that same location. It's made up of five chimes of increasing size (with proportionally decreasing resonating frequency or pitch). Wind movements set chimes in motion so that they may strike each other with varying force, but the larger chimes require a greater force to move and emit sound.

(c) This pentatonic wind chime is augmented with an additional three similar sets of wind chimes. Each set of chimes are made of differing wood or metal material and tuned to a different set of pitches, so that each set of chimes can be aurally distinguished. They are also separated by an X-shaped set of wind-proof walls so wind direction (in each of the four quadrants) as well as force now play a role in which chimes sound.

Would any of the resulting sonic outputs be considered a sonification of wind data? Does the increased information – and deliberate construction – in examples (b) and (c) matter? Do we need to know *why* these devices were made and placed (where we are on the devising continuum) before coming to a conclusion? If (b) and (c) were created just for sonic decoration (not 'auditory scientific visualization') but an attentive listener used it to gain information on changing wind activity, does it change our estimations? What if a researcher used them in a project for 'the purpose of interpreting, understanding, or communicating relations', but no listener gained any knowledge? What if a listener 'incorrectly' hears it as music?

Whatever our answers, let's now consider a rather *Rube Goldbergian* adjustment.

(d) All the chimes are now shielded from the wind, but in each quadrant we place a digital anemometer (wind sensor). Data from these devices is converted in real time to digital information, which is then run through an algorithm that predicts how the chimes would have sounded under these conditions. This in turn triggers a set of mechanical hammers which strike the chimes so as to simulate what would occur naturally.

What has changed? By using an anemometer, we have introduced Scaletti's 'numerically represented relations' into the scenario, albeit at the cost of a ludicrous technological intervention with hammers – one that preserves much of the original mechanism of example (c), though likely at a lower fidelity. Does this new scenario now fall into the category of a sonification? Well, at least the degree of technological intervention shows more purpose. On the other hand, Hermann (2023) argues that the distinction between information and numerical data is irrelevant to broad categorization, for after all, information can always be represented numerically.

Let us try again:

(e) Mercifully, the chimes and their hammers are removed, but the anemometer data is used to trigger MIDI instructions to a sampler instrument, using a similar algorithm to scenario (d). This instrument can convincingly emulate the various original windchimes, but it can equally produce any set of four timbres – yes, even the rustling leaves of (a) but also different pitch sets and spatialized sounds, among other possibilities. The MIDI data can be used in real time or stored for later use and editing, and its tempo can be manipulated, so that, for example, entire days can be played in a few seconds, or a single gust of wind slowed to an hour-long sonic gesture.

Let's suppose that project (e) was set up by a team of meteorological researchers 'R' (perhaps with multiple systems at carefully selected – and sonically spatialised – locations) for the purpose of conveying pertinent weather information to other researchers as part of their arsenal of tools. Weather information might also be filtered down as auditory alerts to local residents (as in a web-based live resource with auditory icons to signal strong easterly winds at these locations). Suppose also that it provided value to the target audience (by providing deeper insight or by attracting widespread use), then it's hard to imagine any commenter *not* classifying this as a bona fide example of data sonification. We might, however, ponder whether the project had to meet *both* conditions – intended purpose and received value – to qualify; or if not, at what point in the progression from examples (a) to (e) the system itself qualified in terms of intervention, complexity, technological or numerical representation.

We are not quite finished. Let's now imagine that the entire project was set up by compositional team C as a tribute to the locale; it is intended, framed and presented as an 'artistic' work (titled *Where the Wind Blows*). Despite its artistic framing, it uses – as creative constraint only – the exact same translation system, underlying data and MIDI output as was used by team R. It is presented as an electronic work and also arranged for orchestra (appropriately spatialised). To counter musical stasis, the composers demarcate times of day and year with modal and textural shifts; they have also added a motif at cyclic intervals, but they have arranged the output so that the motif's modality, instrumental arrangement, dynamic and melodic contour alter according to temperature and other meteorological data. Note that this is all done systematically and no information is altered or lost. With these augmentations we gain musical variety, lose no information and in fact add layers of (objective and systematic) information.

Baxter – with a focus on process, not result – might classify *Where the Wind Blows* as a sonification, but to Neuhoff it is artistic, not empirical sonification. To Scaletti (1994) it seems it is not a sonification at all: even though it has the same system, output (and in the case of the orchestral version) more embedded objective information, it lacks the appropriate purpose and context. What if team R attended the concert, knew the process, recognized and gained insight on the underlying data? Does it now become empirical data sonification despite the absence of the initiating purpose? Alternatively, if the audience knew only the title (and not the process), but sensed and were transported by an impression of familiar flurries, gusts of wind spreading through the orchestral groups, is the underlying data – and information – somehow compromised, lost or incorrect? If the composer, system or orchestra (unwittingly or not) alters, edits, redacts or augments any details, at what point does the sonification degrade or collapse completely?

These questions are not intended to frustrate, but rather to illuminate the complex interweaving and interacting continua of intentions and purpose, musical and empirical listening, technological process, 'faithfulness to the data' and the nature of information embedded within even simple definitions of sonification. Reflecting on these questions adds depth and circumstance to the continuum of initiating purposes (Figure 1: left side), the nature and framing of its reception (right), and how the central sonification process might preserve or distort the relationship between the data and sonic realms. This last issue is the focus of the next section, where the concept of data fidelity is introduced, along with more specific definitions of the translation system.

1.5 Data Fidelity and Hermann's Rules

So far 'sonification' and 'data sonification' have been used rather interchangeably, and indeed the usage by theorists and practitioners tends to be blurry and subject to no universal standard. If we take *data* to mean 'anything that isn't (yet) sound' then the 'data' prefix becomes somewhat redundant, however if 'data' means anything more than 'anything' (implying, for example, purpose, objectivity and systematic processes) then a distinction must exist. While Baxter's (2020) emphasis of the verbal noun form of sonification sidesteps questions of data identification, some theorists use 'sonification' as a shorthand for 'data sonification', to which specific criteria are attached. While I don't aim to prescribe a standardised terminology and further clutter the wilderness of terminologies, I find it useful to take *sonification* in its most general sense, covering any possible translation into sound. *Data sonification* is more specific: the term *data* has implications for the source material, its collection and the nature and fidelity of the translation (where fidelity means both faithfulness and resolution).

Let us illustrate the distinction with an example. The melody of Arvo Pärt's *Spiegel im Spiegel* ('Mirror in Mirror') might be thought of as a sonification – as in 'sonic translation' – of a systematic reflection of scale degrees either side, and in alternating directions from and to a central pitch. It is not a *data* sonification, as the melody was not collected from objective observations (or algorithmic representations) of objects in reflection. But it is in fact physically realisable with two movable mirrors, and if we created a similar piece through data collection of these reflections mapped to scale degrees, then perhaps it might be considered an example of data sonification. To what degree (if at all) different compositional strategies – algorithmic, process, generative and so forth – meet the criteria of sonification (with or without the data prefix) I leave to the reader now that we have at least acknowledged the tangled continua. To complicate matters further, Scaletti suggests that (apparently all) music is itself a strictly defined sonification – of musical thought. It is a 'morphism, a cross-domain, inference-preserving mapping from thought to sound ... a sonification of what it's like to be inside our heads ... like mind-melding with the person who created the music' (Scaletti, 2021:383).[13] This is indicated in Figure 1 as 'Scaletti's morphism'. In Section 3.2, we shall return to the nature of music and sonic communication, and we shall consider how this claim might be resolved in generative, ambiguous, algorithmic and indeed data music when there is no clear identifiable mind with which to meld.

Let us now turn to the question of data fidelity: how might we assess to what extent the sonification process is true to the data? This question becomes easier to think about if we make an analogy with data graphics. Consider, for example, a bar graph of life expectancy in various populations across the last 100 years then – so long as we have a robust methodology of data collection, and this data is placed faithfully on labelled axes – we have a valid data visualisation.[14] We can identify patterns and compare eras and populations with specificity and without ambiguity. On our graph, we might colour the data sets for clarity and strive for a functional visual beauty. We might even (systematically) round some numbers or design the graph so that exact figures are not clearly visible without losing an objective fidelity. If however, we start manipulating, fudging or excluding numbers, or obfuscate the visual presentation of the graph, then we compromise our fidelity (and, if the work is published, become susceptible to accusations of disinformation and malpractice). So too with a sonic graph, where life expectancy might be connected to a range of pitches over a timeline of the changing generations. We may 'colour' the data timbrally for aesthetic satisfaction or enhanced listening (or both) and a wide range of numbers might be scaled and rounded to a reasonably informative subset of pitches. However, if the input data (or its direct sonification) is manipulated or obfuscated by the conversion system or the canvas, our fidelity is compromised. Although the output might be termed data-driven or data-inspired music, it is

---

[13] Scaletti's description of musical communication as 'mind-melding' is incidentally reminiscent of the seminal linguist Sapir's 1921 description of language as the 'mold of thought' (Sapir, 2014:117)

[14] For an examination of how the graphic realm can be manipulated to present information in a misleading way, see Tufte (2001).

not the 'the auditory equivalent of scientific visualization' and should not be presented as such. This is not to say that there is a perfect data sonification system and anything that falls short is useless: this fidelity exists on a continuum and can vary within a sonic presentation itself. It is perfectly reasonable, if articulated, to select from data to provide illustrations and 'fair representations' of processes and data sets. Data can, of course, also be used to a greater or lesser extent as part of the compositional process as a tribute, inspiration, creative constraint or stimulus. But what are the criteria for data fidelity and how might we assess to what extent a project is 'true to the data' rather than 'composition using data material'?

My thinking on this topic is informed by Hermann's definitions of sonification on the sonification.de website (Hermann, 2023), as well as by a recurring theme in the seminal *Sonification Handbook* (Hermann et al., 2011) hosted there:

> *Any technique that uses data as input, and generates (eventually only in response to additional excitation or triggering) sound signals may be called sonification, if and only if*
>
> *(A) the sound reflects properties / relations in the input data.*
> *(B) the transformation is completely systematic. This means that there is a precise definition of how interactions and data cause the sound to change.*
> *(C) the sonification is reproducible: given the same data and identical interactions/triggers the resulting sound has to be structurally identical.*
> *(D) the system can intentionally be used with different data, and also be used in repetition with the same data.* (Hermann, 2010)

Hermann also offers a short definition of sonification as 'the data-dependent generation of sound, if the transformation is systematic, objective and reproducible, so that it can be used as scientific method'. This comes with useful discussions offering answers to the relationship between 'information' and data'; irrelevant, he says, as the former can be represented numerically. These definitions also suggest that project (a) (see Section 1.4) is a sonification if we believe that the rustling leaves are receiving additional 'external data input', and not otherwise. Practically, they offer clear guidelines for composition that can be variously adopted or consciously rejected.

As a concise tool for the practice and teaching of sonification I have adapted Hermann's definitions into 'Hermann's Rules' or 'four Rs':

R1) **rule-based** (data is translated systematically)
R2) **repeatable** (if the process is repeated with the same data set, it produces the same results)

R3) **relevant** (pertinent and relevant data of the 'domain under study' is selected), and

R4) **recognisable** (significant patterns in, and differences within or between data sets are recognised sonically/musically)

We might add a fifth R, **reason**, which would require the project to have an appropriate purpose (so that the rustling leaves or 'decorative wind chimes' would no longer qualify as sonifications). Again, these rules all operate on continua (how exact do repetitions need to be, how precise the recognisability – and to whom?) that could be used to identify thresholds of success. A project (and its component data streams) may variously meet some but not all of Hermann's four Rs. For example Villa-Lobos's *New York Skyline Melody* meets all four when tracing the simultaneous contours of the skyline, but adds a layer of dynamics and harmony to make these sonified melodies 'work'.[15] This 'data scoring' disobeys the first three rules: (1) the rules governing it are not fixed a priori; (2) it is not repeatable, for if the skyline changed, so would the principles behind the scoring; (3) the scoring is not relevant to the domain under study. Still, collectively we would likely recognise from the 'relevant' melodic contours a host of different skylines. This work would not meet Hermann's 'if and only if' sonification definition, but meets many of the component Rs, delegating, as it does, a significant portion of its compositional content to an external data source.

Now that we have discussed the various threads of the sonification continuum and even have some rules to work with, we are ready to focus on the translation system and specific techniques for the sonic representation of data.

2 The Sonification Process

2.1 Models of Translation

Section 1 was concerned with the relationship between data and sound, with particular emphasis on continua and the concept of data fidelity. To examine how these concerns might operate in the practical construction of a translation system, we can use as a subject the traditional practice of *musical cryptogram*, the conversion of extra-musical text (usually letters of a name) to musical symbols (note names or rhythmic units). The most common usage of musical cryptogram has been by Western composers (including J. S. Bach, Schumann, Ravel, Shostakovich, Liszt, Oliveros, Messiaen, Takemitsu, Elgar and many others) to form musical motifs as a ciphered personal tribute to themselves or

---

[15] This is analogous to Tufte's concept of 'chart junk' in data visualisation (see Tufte (2021)).

others (Sams, 1980). Other systems, though originally steganographic,[16] are also adopted in compositional use, such as the Morse code signals (the translation of letters to patterns of short-long rhythmic units), employed in the studio practice of Delia Derbyshire (Langton, 2020). Depending on definitions, not all of these systems and uses would completely satisfy our sonification criteria or the four Rs, but they might be made to, and they are nonetheless instructive in how they fail to do so.

Returning to our vision of sonification as the passing of information from the data to the sonic realms (see again Figure 1), let's zoom in to the point of transformation and examine what is happening to the data itself. We might, for example, imagine an idealised translation system where any data point (be it a letter in a text, or a level of wind pressure and direction) has a unique sonic output (say a note name, a rhythmic pattern or the frequency of a low-pass filter). In this case we can consider that the system is *isomorphic*. The translation process changes the language but preserves the structure and resolution of the data. We could then (and in the case of Morse code, are conventionally expected to) reverse the process so that the original signal can be rebuilt without error. This *transparent* translation model is illustrated (in a generalised form) in the top left of Figure 2, where every data point (and every set of data points) has a corresponding unique sonic output, in an invertible one-to-one correspondence. The arrow of sonification can run in both directions: We know the precise sonic output a data set will produce, and the input data behind every sonic output. If we limit our data domain to letters (excluding cases) then International Morse Code (which has a unique and isolated rhythmic pattern for every case-neutral letter)[17] achieves this isomorphism.

Now let's take the same data domain (of case-neutral letters) and examine how the original 'German' system of cryptogram (which produces the BACH motif) holds up. In this system the first eight letters of the alphabet are linked to the eight note names of the German notation system (again A through H, although 'B' in German music nomenclature is a common-practice B♭, and 'H' a B♮). While Bach enjoyed a completely translatable surname, letters from I onwards are 'lost in translation'. Augmentations to the system included mapping letters phonetically – for example 'S' is linked to E♭ (as 'Es' is the German term for that note) – but some cryptograms remained 'gapped': Brahms, for instance, only managed a four-note motif (BAHS) from his surname, while Dimitri Shostakovich adopted the musical signature DSCH, derived from the German spelling of his name, D. Schostakovich). So

---

[16] For a succinct but comprehensive survey of musical encryption see Code (2023).
[17] See ITU (2009).

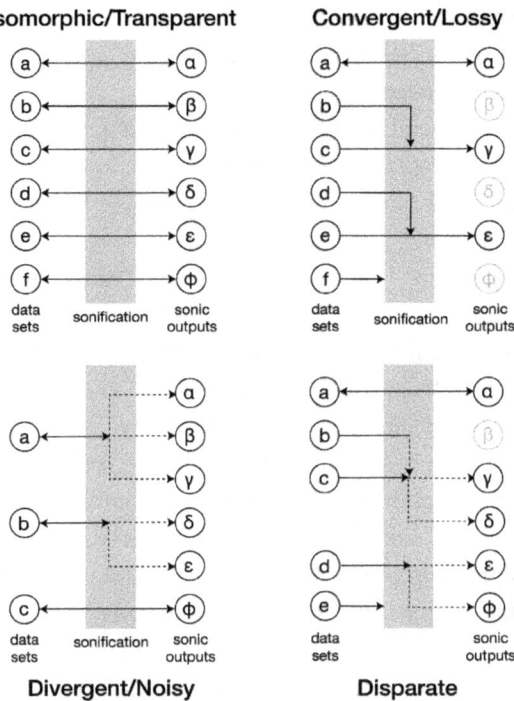

Figure 2 Four illustrations of how data sets and sonic outputs may be related in the sonification process.

although it is rule-based, the German system is 'lossy' in that data is lost in conversion and we can't confidently rebuild the input data from the sonic output (for example, 'I know Bach' and 'Bach' yield the same four-note melody).

Under this German system, few names can be ciphered in their entirety: gapping is usually unavoidable. To obtain additional letters, some composers drew on the note names used in traditional solfège, where C–D–E ... is sung as do–re–mi .... Supposing we wanted to cipher the letters RLM: then the letter R = re = the note D; letter L = la = the note A; the letter M = mi = the note E, and so on. This expedient, however, introduced convergence in the system, for now letters such as D and R would result in the same musical note name output. Even so, some letters are not accounted for. The 'French system' of cryptograms addressed these gaps in the letter domain: it 'wraps round' the mappings of (A-G, H-N, O-U and V-Z), so that A, H, O and U all map to the musical note A; B, I, P and V to the note B and so on. What is gained in terms of letter coverage comes at the cost of considerable convergence: everyone's name gets a complete melody but some melodies are shared. This lossiness or convergence is inevitable when the number of possible inputs (26 letters) outnumber the possible outputs (eight German note names). Figure 2 (top right) illustrates this lossiness and convergence.

Convergence in general sonification is also an outcome of *quantization* where pitches, rhythms and other parameters may be rounded. For example, we might quantize a microtonal line to 12 equal divisions of the octave, 'free timed' events to their nearest rhythmic subdivisions, a wide range of amplitude to a set of dynamic markings, and so on. This rounding of various musical dimensions to a lattice of rational musical divisions (see Wishart 1996) is usually undertaken for the sake of musical accessibility and notational economy, but the data fidelity (as in 'resolution') is diminished. The translation process of a convergent system creates a more pixelated form of the original data (at either the data pre-processing or sonic post-processing stage), but the payoff in sonification is considerable: an increase in accessibility, perception and (in terms of composition) flexibility of the sonic material.

In cryptographic composition the composer is conventionally allowed to choose the octave register in which each note name is realised and to insert additional (harmonic or connective) pitches to support the emerging melody. Chromatic alterations of the note-names are also sometimes allowed. While it may still be possible to rebuild the input source from a melody – despite this additional licence – the system is now *divergent*: it adds noise (or, more positively, 'creative freedom') to the input, so that we cannot predict the sonic output from a given input in all its detail. To put it another way, *divergence* means that we cannot state a set of systematic rules to explain how the sonic output is derived from the given input. While a divergent translation still preserves some or most of the information, it places a greater burden on the listener to retrace the original data, since the scope of sonic outputs *exceeds* that of the input data. Data can also be obfuscated by such divergence; Villa-Lobos added harmonic support to his sonified skyline of New York, and a faithful retracing would render additional architectural lines to the reconstructed image. If we wished for the original image to be sonically preserved, we might arrange Villa-Lobos's solo piano work for piano and strings, one instrumental group faithfully rendering the skyline contours, the other providing 'data scoring'. An illustration of a divergent system is presented in Figure 2 (lower left).

Systems can also exhibit both convergence and divergence: components of a data set may variously be lost, converge through quantization, and diverge from their particular sources. Such a disparate system may introduce anywhere from a subtle or extreme interference between data input and sonic output. Multiple data streams might even exhibit isomorphism, divergence and convergence simultaneously. For example, a series of temperatures with coordinates and timestamps: the temperatures might encode exactly; the coordinates might be quantized; the timestamps might diverge through the random addition of harmonies.

Let's now consider how we might counter such distortions and modify a cryptogram system so that it exhibits isomorphism, a one-to-one correspondence of the twenty-six letters to a useful pitch set. We will try to do this with the French system explained earlier. One option would be to use octave register to accommodate the remaining letters: we map A–G onto their musical namesakes starting just below middle C; next, we map H–N onto A–G, an octave above; and so on. Every letter now has its own pitch (if not pitch class).[18] Should we wish to map to chromatic notes then the twenty-six letters will occupy just over two octaves of note space. In fact, a comprehensive letter-note isomorphic system can be co-opted from the ASCII (American Standard Code for Information Interchange) set, which assigns an eight-bit code to common keyboard characters, including case-sensitive letters, digits, punctuation marks and formatting commands. These 128 characters map conveniently to the 128 MIDI pitches, thus preserving complete fidelity in translation. Should we wish to, a formatted book (like this one) could be completely encoded in 'melodic' material.

Figure 3 now recapitulates all of the systems just described. It shows how the same text material – using various cryptographic systems – is encoded musically, and how it would be decoded back to the data realm.

The traditional use of cryptogram is to pay tribute by generating musical material that would not exist without – and is apparently unique to – the dedicatee. As for the composer, it provides them with both a stimulus and a valuable creative constraint. In general, however, cryptogram is used only as a constraint; it does not necessarily dictate the broad language, style and structure of the work. (There are, of course, some exceptions, such as Oliveros's meditative *CAGE DEAD* and Arvo Pärt's *Collage über B-A-C-H*: in these two pieces, cryptographic material is sustained and foregrounded.)

I happen to enjoy employing cryptographic material in my work – for example, in improvisation, creative constraints and ad hoc live demonstrations. For the ciphering process, I often make use of *Crypto*, a software patch I designed and built with Phelan Kane (see Section 3.1.10) that can take input from a text file or computer keyboard and translate it to MIDI notes in real

---

[18] The traditional and 'wrapped' version of the French System are named in Figure 3 French (press) and French (wrap) respectively.

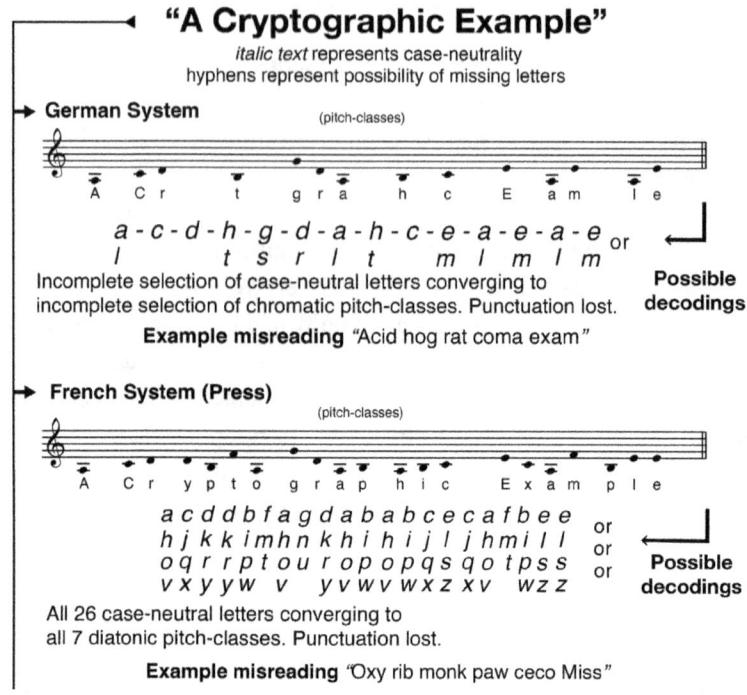

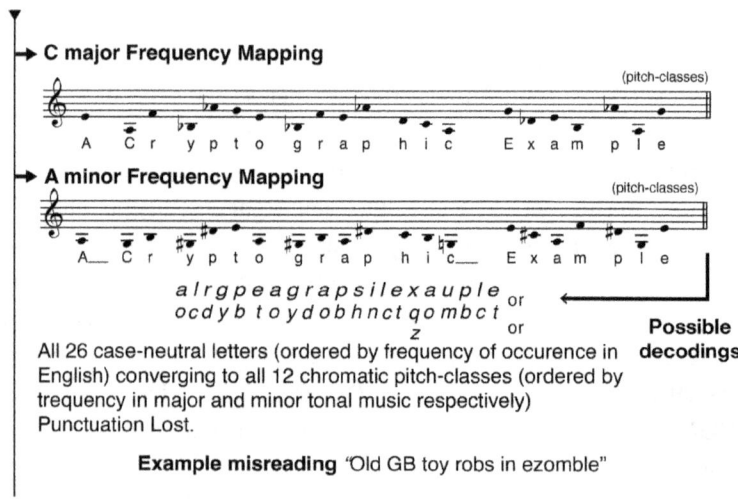

Figure 3 The phrase 'A Cryptographic Example' is translated through various historic and novel translation systems. Pitch, pitch-class and, in the case of International Morse Code, rhythmic outputs are shown. Below each system there is an illustration of how reliably (or otherwise) the original message can be decoded. Note the high degree of lossiness and convergence in the traditional German and French systems, compared to the precision of ASCII and International Morse Code. Phonetic percussion and frequency mapping provide more 'meaning' in syllabic shape and melodic characteristics respectively.

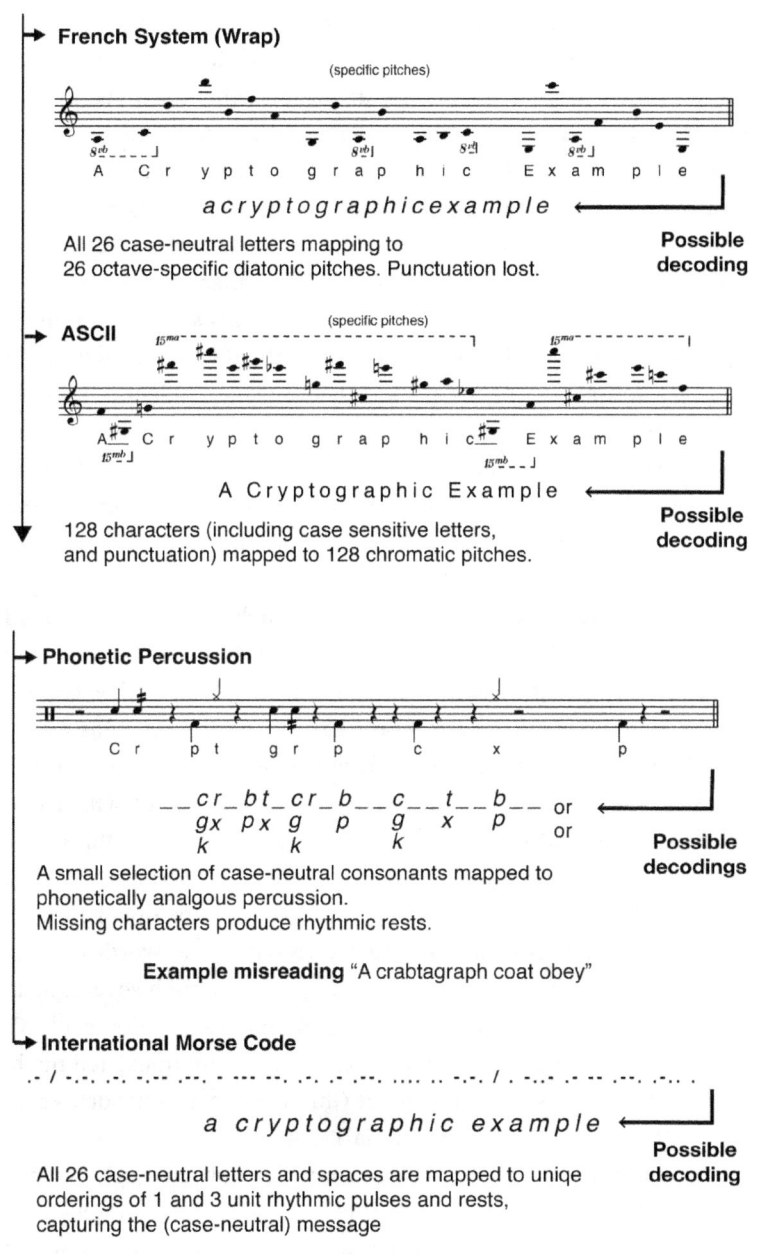

Figure 3 (cont.)

time. Sometimes a piece is made up entirely of cryptographic material (including rhythmic as well as pitch translations), while in other works the cryptographic material is just that: hidden away, an undisclosed (though discoverable) message or joke – and largely of personal value.

Depending on how much of the translation system is isomorphic, we *might* learn to recognise repeated words, letter frequency and even languages, but the *specific* letter-to-pitch mappings in the systems discussed so far, are inherently arbitrary. The sonic translation might carry the information, but is it *conveyed* (i.e., received by the listener)? How, then, might we gain a deeper sonic communication out of the text itself – not just the message in an alien language but a comprehensible representation of its content? One approach I've taken is to map consonants to phonetically similar drum kit sounds (such as the plosives *p* and *b* to kick drum; hard consonants *k*, *g* and *q* to the snare; *r* to drum rolls; *t* and *x* to hi hat; and so on. With other letters acting as rests, 'chokes' or resonants, phrases like 'boom-tish', 'didactic cactus' and 'Tumtum tree' produce convincingly satisfying rhythmic patterns. Another approach I've devised is not phonetic, but maps letter frequency to the frequency of pitch-class occurrences in tonal music. For example common letters like *E* and *T* (see Lewand, 2000) would map to the commonly occurring pitch-classes in a key (such as E and A in the key of A minor – see Huron, 2008), and rare letters like *Q* and *Z* to the rarer pitch classes (e.g. C♯ and B♭ in the key of A minor). While this is a rudimentary (and convergent) mapping (which in its current state avoids bigrams, trigrams and other contexts) it produces satisfying results where words like 'ease' produce consonance and 'quixotic' a non-diatonic angularity. It also (for me at least) introduces to conventional compositional strategies a direct engagement with frequency distribution of musical events. A piece may be generated with an a priori uneven rationing of various musical materials that can be balanced throughout a work: relative frequency becomes a guiding compositional mechanism, rather than a passive outcome of 'free' creativity. It is worth returning to Figure 3 here. As we have seen, it runs one phrase through several historical and novel musical cryptographic systems, to demonstrate the level of 'data fidelity' given convergence (such as when letters share translated pitched or have no mapped pitches) and divergence (through non-specific octaves, or the allowance of additional melodic material).

This section has focused on cryptogram, which conventionally maps case-neutral letters to diatonic or chromatic pitch-classes. Our discussion soon led to the notion of convergence. We then saw that attempts to better map these twenty-six data points to seven or twelve pitch classes invite the expansion of the sonic domain to octave-identified pitches (as opposed to octave-neutral pitches). This allows extra capacity (let's say three octaves of chromatic notes) to capture all letters, and even expand the data domain to include case-sensitive letters and punctuation. Musical parameters (even when quantized) have copious capacity for data storage: for example, different timbres (or instruments), dynamics and rhythmic values can be attached to pitches, and so the sonifier can adjust the scope of the sonic domain to best accommodate the given data domain.

As we have seen, embedding data in this way might spur and constrain a composer's creativity in fruitful ways; it also fulfils the repeatability and rule-base of Hermann's 4 Rs. However, cryptogram may not (and usually doesn't) meet Hermann's other criteria of relevance or recognizability (or the underlying project reason). As a result, it may not effectively communicate meaningful information about text or language and thus may not meet the hard criteria for data sonification. It could be made to, perhaps, through the use of frequency-mapping, or a more nuanced speech-aware treatment of text through phonemes. Nonetheless, this exploration of cryptogram has allowed us to consider how a particular system maps any data domain to sonic parameters, taking into account the fidelity of the translation and how compositional freedom might relate to such fidelity. If we are mapping letters, are they case sensitive, and are pitches 'octave-sensitive'? If not a one-to-one correspondent isomorphism, what are the acceptable levels of convergence and divergence, and how – if at all – can the data be rebuilt from its sonic translation? If, say, tracing the contour of a coastline to a melodic line, what is an acceptable degree of 'pixelation', and how precisely and clearly can a listener recognize and retrace the source material from its sonic representation? What is the scope of the data set (all letters, temperatures, blood types, traffic events, etc.) and sonic output (pitch or pitch class, chromatic completion, parameter range, etc.)? To what extent can the sonified data be coloured and augmented, without obfuscating the signal? This balance of creative constraint, data fidelity, flexibility of material and information conveyance make up much of the data composer's craft.

2.2 Classifications and the Analogic–Symbolic Continuum

The sonification community has adopted a commonly accepted set of data translation methods, and agreed on various terms, including auditory icons, earcons, audification, parametric mapping, discrete versus continuous mapping, "ReMapping" (Gresham-Lancaster & Sinclair, 2012), interactive sonic graphs and model-based sonification. Many of these are outlined in technical detail in *The Sonification Handbook* (Herman et al., 2011), while a succinct, accessible overview is presented by Worrall (2011). Rather than provide immediate definitions, this section again takes a ground-up exploration of how data can be represented so that we can actively discover – rather than passively receive – these strategies. A very useful starting point is Kramer's (1994) concept of an analogic versus symbolic continuum, where at one end of the continuum, sound is generated as an 'intrinsic ... simple analogue' (Kramer, 1994:21) to the input data. Examples might include data of the Earth's vertical motion from a seismometer translated to a pressure wave in the audio domain, a Geiger counter's sonification of radiation level by the periodicity of clicks, or the gamma frequency band of EEG data 'writing' the acoustic signal. With some tools, such as a sonogram or oscillogram, we can quite literally see the data embedded in the audio domain.

On the other end of the continuum, symbolic mappings translate data to the acoustic signal more indirectly, and can be thought of as discrete, independent and arbitrary sonic 'triggers' associated with a data event or value. These include the ping of a microwave, a smoke alarm siren, or an audio sample (let's say, an electric piano playing E∆/C) that sounds when the UV index exceeds 2. The resulting audio is connected *symbolically* to the data, but its sonic identity is otherwise unrelated (although it might include metaphorical connotations). Through symbolic representation we might learn *about* the data domain, so long as we knew or could intuit the 'key' to the symbols – the underlying schema or external set of rules governing the sonic event. Conversely, in analogic representation, the structure of the data is in some sense reflected *inside* the sonic translation. One might think of analogic representation as the data *inscribing* the acoustic signal (usually with a level of processing, such as scaling to the audio spectrum), and symbolic representation as the data *instructing* the sounding of a number of discrete and independent sonic events. Worrall's (2011:315) observation of the Greek derivation of the prefixes and suffixes of *ana-logic* ('upon-form') and *sym-bolic* ('together-gather') is particularly illuminating when considering the relationship between the data and the sonic realms.

The degree to which a sound is 'derived directly from the data' has been given the term indexicality (Barrass & Vickers, 2011:157), with directly derived sound indicating high indexicality, and more symbolic representations having low indexicality. At the highest level/degree of indexicality – and on the leftmost position on the analogue-symbolic continuum – lies audification, which is 'the direct translation of a data waveform to the audible domain' (Worrall, 2011:321). Such a translation typically requires a large number of data points, with a high enough sample rate for a continuous data waveform to be made audible. Then some type of filtering or processing – processed audification – may be necessary: for instance, seismographic data must be sped up to be audified.[19] In this way a data waveform can be transposed (in both senses) to the audio domain. For an illustration, let's imagine that we are on a pier looking out to sea. Using a camera

---

[19] See Dombois & Eckel, 2011:301–320.

or sensor, we take rapid samples of the height of the sea surface. The resulting data set would correspond to the sea's waves, resulting in waveforms of varying height, rate and shape. This method of measurement would simplify breaking waves, but would capture a linear wave-height over time. Anyone familiar with electronic music can imagine how an extreme transposition (say five octaves higher) of this wave-height-over-time of the data to the amplitude-over-time of an oscillator could make changes in sea conditions audible – silent (no waves), slow large waves (low pitch, loud), fast ripples (high pitch, quiet) and so on. The timbre would vary expressively in accordance with wave shape (which for ocean waves generally ranges from the smooth sine curve to the more pointed trochoid (see Mayo, 1997)), as well as additional noise from wind and other external factors. In Figure 1, audification is shown as an arrow straight from the data set to the audio domain. For ocean waves, audification would require speeding up the time scale – a day of waves would be shrunk to a few minutes in the audio domain. Alternatively, we could time-stretch back to a real-time representation by repeating, interpolating and updating the waveform. It would be possible to hear the actual shape of the wave contours in real time (or any tempo) if – instead of inscribing the audio signal directly – we used it to control some sonic parameter (like volume, pitch, cutoff frequency, melodic range etc.) of a carrier signal, such as a sustained timbre. This parameter-mapping approach – a central technique in data-music – is (in Kramer's model) less 'direct' than audification, but still 'carries' the data (and oceanic) wave.

At the symbolic end of the continuum (and with low indexicality) one might consider how a data event is the *least* directly associated with a sound. Take the idea of a sonic alarm, triggered when an event occurs or a threshold is met in the data realm. In sonification practice, these are given the term *auditory icons* (see Brazil & Fernström, 2011): they are associated particularly with user interfaces, as in the paper rustle of a deleted file or the sad pitch drop of an exhausted Bluetooth device. The played audio samples inform us of the world, but the sonic material, which may or not be evocative of its target, stands in for a data event. The high level of symbolism (or low indexicality) of auditory icons is usually associated with *discrete* data points: a singular event or state is linked to a single sonic object. Thus, symbolic representations (and low indexicality) are generally best suited to discrete data representations, as opposed to the continuity of data that is necessary to feed and represent audification. Indexicality and continuity are not equivalent terms. We can opt to mark specific levels of a continuous data stream with unconnected sonic objects; equally, auditory icons might interrelate despite having no direct-to-sound components, such as a scale built from a cryptogram – there is little, if any, meaningful continuity in the data set, but the translation to pitches produces a sense of continuity.

Icons can even have their own syntax to form *earcons*. Imagine, for example, a sonic communication of your phone's battery, Wi-Fi and cellular status. For each of these three features, there is a sound with its own identity (say an industrial 'power' noise, a cloud-like pad and an eight-bit burst, respectively). A 'full' status plays the appropriate sample directly, but lower levels (of battery charge, and Wi-Fi and cellular strength) alter each individual sample using various pitch and dynamic effects. The result is a shared sonic language of symbolic auditory icons, here used to indicate level and issue calls for attention. Though conventionally associated with user interfaces, this concept makes for a useful strategy in data composition. Imagine an accelerated time-line representation of global conflicts over a historical period, where each war is given its own motivic icon. The start, peak and end of each war are given distinguishing dynamic, arranging and modal characteristics, so that although the wars are represented by distinct sonic objects, there is a shared syntax providing information about the individual state of each.

As with so many of the concepts we have studied so far, analogic and symbolic representation do not make a binary classification: they lie in a continuum. In fact, they can be used simultaneously, mixing strategies for individual data streams or even within the same data stream, such as a seismometer's continuous 'smooth' indication of geological activity coupled with discrete auditory 'alerts' that sound once a certain threshold is met.[20] Furthermore, most sonification strategies (particularly in artistic practice) approach the data somewhere between 'pure' analogic and entirely symbolic representation: the most common and flexible instance of this is *parameter mapping*, where the data (or simultaneous streams of data) control any number of characteristics of an acoustic signal or musical object.

For an illustration, let's create a 'temperature melody' by mapping environmental temperature to the sound of a violin (acoustic or sampled). We will do it so that the fundamental frequency of each violin tone is 'upon the form' of the temperature, using a logarithmic scale where a difference of 1°C is equivalent to approximately one semitone (i.e., approximately 5.95% difference in frequency). Although this decision likely entails some convergence, the data structure will be retained to some extent. Our melody certainly illustrates analogic representation: temperature values are inscribed directly onto the audio signal. But other components of the melody are symbolic. After all, the violin timbre itself has been *assigned* the role of (or gathered together with) temperature. To be sure, there

---

[20] Practically speaking, one might appreciate a smoke alarm equipped with two settings: a quieter alarm that sounds at a lower threshold (reminding us to open a window or start the fan during cooking) and the full siren that is emitted when the usual threshold is met: a sliver of continuity added to the usually discrete auditory icon.

might be perceptual and functional reasons for the choice of violin: the listener can segregate it from other data-streams (or contextual scoring); it can be sustained indefinitely; it allows microtonal as well as stepped pitches; and it might provide a suitable range for the data set, given the translation method described. Furthermore, it allows additional information layering. Alongside the temperature melody, independent notes might be added (such as the introduction of an occasional drone open string); bowing techniques and dynamics can be modified. In this way, a single violin can potentially carry more data (by virtue of possessing more information capacity): temperature translates to pitch as described, but also UV index to volume, periods of rainfall to a drone open string and humidity to mellowness (on the violin, an increased distance between bow and bridge). We can even use multiple parameters to display one data stream: as temperature increases, so can both pitch and loudness, reinforcing the 'signal'. These mapping strategies between data and sonic streams can run in parallel (temperature to pitch, rainfall to drone) or in a one-to-many configuration (temperature to both pitch *and* volume) or many-to-one (e.g. a measure of rainfall combined with a measure of humidity to reverberation). Beyond its raw information-carrying capability, the symbolic choice of a violin may not be completely arbitrary. There could be metaphorical (geographical, aesthetic or sentimental) reasons behind the choice of instruments or even behind the choice of its component data streams – UV index is 'intense' and low humidity is 'dry'. Parameter mapping can be abstracted endlessly: for example, temperature could be used to control any feature, such as the volume, harmony or tempo of an independent musical object (like a motif or complete track) – a 'side-chained' parameter mapping.

A representation of the 'analogic-symbolic continuum' is presented in Figure 4b, with the illustrative (but not specific) position of several sonification methods along the continuum. Let us now demonstrate some of these methods with a practical example: sonifying a heartbeat.

2.3 The Heart of the Matter: A Map of Mappings

While the analogic-symbolic continuum – and level of indexicality – address the directness of data representation, they should not be confused with data fidelity, nor with how effectively information is eventually received by the listener. That is to say, although an analogic representation is more direct, a symbolic abstraction may make it through the various boundaries between the data realm and the listener more reliably: even if fewer data points reach the listener, more information may be preserved. Some data sets might invite a particular sonification method: for example, continuous data sampled at a high rate may be a good candidate for audification, while occasional events may be best portrayed with auditory icons. However – as will be shown here – even apparently simple data sets allow a range of approaches from continuous to discrete, and analogic to symbolic. We can think of the analogic-symbolic continuum (see Figure 4b) as the central sonification membrane of Figure 1. Data must pass through it in some way, many approaches are open to the sonifier, and each illuminates and draws into focus characteristics of the underlying information.

Take, for example, the data set of a human heartbeat. Our everyday engagement with this measure is in terms of pulses per minute (which – as it happens – maps in terms of range and concept to that of musical tempo). But heart rate is itself an abstraction of a more complex underlying data source. Figure 4a shows the author's own ECG (with a thankfully normal sinus rhythm), self-administered at the time of writing and shortly after a coffee. It shows a rate of around 72 bpm (about 1.2 Hz). This value is calculated as a measure between peaks (labelled R) in the heartbeat pattern (this measure from one R to the next is called the RR interval). With a simple calculation, the RR interval determines the heart rate[21] and its range and regularity over time, but says nothing of the wave shape between the RR intervals. But now, as with our oceanic wave, let's take this continuous data source and, by speeding it up – or, in musical terms, transposing it – bring it into the domain of pitch. Changes in the BPM are now heard as a fundamental pitch change, and the wave shape between the R peaks alters the harmonic characteristics of the resulting timbre This is the audification approach shown in Figure 4b.

But there is also a way for us to engage with the inner structure of the heartbeat, just as a cardiologist uses its shape to diagnose heart function. Alongside the R peaks, the contour is given various additional points (PQS and T R) – with relative intervals and sections (such as the PR Interval) – which allows a better understanding of heart function within the heartbeat and the nature of the 'ba-dum' asymmetry. This PQRST complex is tantalisingly reminiscent of the AHDSR (Attack Hold Decay Sustain Release), ADSR and other envelope generators used in audio synthesis. And indeed as in audio synthesis, this heartbeat contour could be used as an envelope to modulate any parameter such as the amplitude, or the cut-off filter of a harmonically rich oscillator source.[22] Figure 4g shows a generalised form of this mapping of the contour against some continuous parameter, which might be volume, panning, or cut-off frequency of the carrier signal. This signal is selected to respond well to such modifications (it might even be the heart-rate audification itself). The contour

---

[21] If the RR interval is measured in ms, BPM = 60000/(RR).
[22] The discovery of such physical world-to-sonic analogues has become an important and rewarding aspect of the sonification craft.

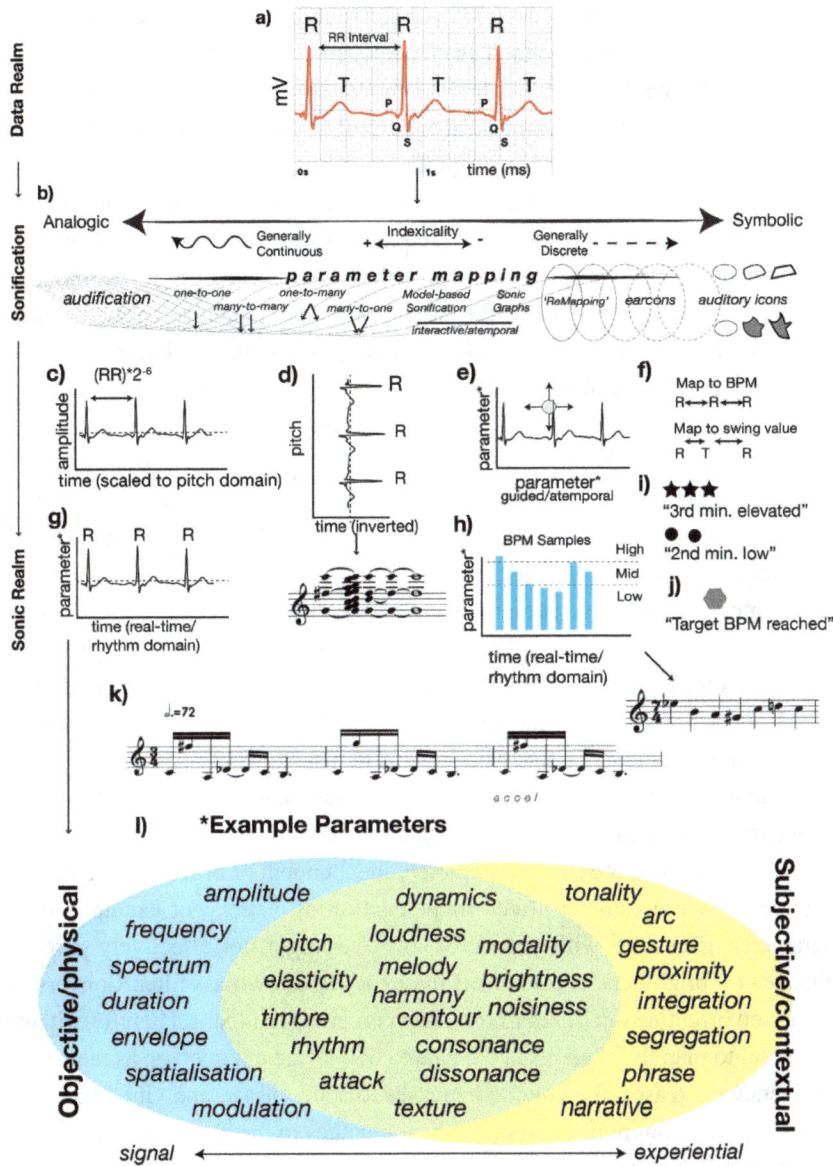

Figure 4 An illustration of some sonification techniques in relation to the analogic-to-symbolic continuum. An example data source (a human heartbeat) (a) is run through various points of the (b) analogic-to-symbolic continuum, resulting in a variety of sonifications (c–k). Some example parameter mappings are also shown (l).

might be used to dictate the level of any continuous parameter such as volume, pan position pan, or a monophonic pitch contour – such as a theremin swoop, or it might be 'pixelated' onto musical staff notation, as in Villa-Lobos's skyline.

This ECG curve, then, can be used to control any sonic parameter of a signal. For example, we can control the signal's brightness (by controlling the cut-off frequency or resonance of a low-pass filter), its gain, or its position in sonic space; we can use it to govern the frequency of an oscillator in the pitch or rhythmic domain; if we apply an effect to the signal, its level could change with the curve; finally, we could use the curve to inscribe a melody, which could be 'smooth' or quantized in pitch, rhythm or both (see Figure 4k). These changes to properties in the signal variously affect the listener's experience of contour, dissonance, consonance and cohesion in multiple musical parameters. In this way, the listener might make sense of the data set in terms of how it changes – and interacts with other data streams – over time, forming trajectories and arcs. This continuum from objective manipulations of the signal and the listener's experience is illustrated in Figure 4l.

Parameter mapping is a supremely useful and efficient tool in sonification, for it allows the carrying of multiple data streams in relatively simple sonic textures: A tone dropping in pitch with a widening and slowing vibrato, travelling from left to right in the stereo field and receding into the reverberated distance manages to carry five data streams in just one continuous voice. At the same time, parameter mapping also presents challenges in precise information conveyance, not only because it can ask too much of human perception but also because parameters are rarely completely independent or orthogonal: crucially, changes in one parameter affect the perception of others. For example, if the parameter associated with volume is low, we might not effectively perceive changes to 'brightness' – the cut-off frequency of a low-pass filter. Conversely, increased brightness in a signal can affect perceived loudness. Therefore, it may be useful to map the changes in the data to both these parameters: as the cut-off frequency decreases, the volume increases to compensate, and vice versa. This 'one-to-many' mapping allows us to hear changes in the data as a composite of parameters. We can also represent multiple data streams in one parameter – for example, our spatial or pitch dimension might be 'zoned out' to multiple data streams – in a 'many-to-one' configuration. Parameter mapping is a particularly useful sonification technique when representing processes – when levels in properties of the data set change over time. A process is successfully represented when the listener perceives both continuity and change. Thus, if we visualise the information as creating a grid in which the property being measured runs vertically and time runs horizontally, then the grid must have enough vertical gridlines to reveal continuity in the data and enough horizontal gridlines to convey change. When these conditions are met, the result is a contour – with the impression of continuity – that is analogous to the data. This kind of contour will be quite familiar to anyone engaged with, say, the automation curves of a DAW or MIDI mapping of control parameters in live electronics – or, for that matter, the expressive contours of gestures in sonic art (Wishart, 1996: 93–104) or in jazz analysis and pedagogy (Mermikides & Feygelson, 2017). All the same, however familiar and accessible the concept, the mapping possibilities and challenges in effective communication are countless and non-trivial.

My work happens to make extensive and varied use of parameter mapping, but – through an engagement with musical analysis – it has developed to include what might be termed *higher-level mapping*. With this term I refer to a way of working in which the raw parameters of the signal – pitch, timbre and rhythm – are manipulated in such a way as to produce an *emergent* parameter. Some examples:

- degree of harmonic consonance or dissonance (derived through a weighted expression of interval vector (Mermikides, 2022a)
- modal brightness, from the nocturnal Locrian to the radiant Lydian (Mermikides, 2022b)
- level of syncopation, through weighted beat placements and rests
- complexity of ratio in rhythmic grouping or just intonation, harmonicity (a sine wave morphing to a sawtooth wave in a wavetable) and *proximity* in the cycle of fifths, tonnetz space,
- motivic or sonic transformation in multiple dimensions (Mermikides, 2010:27–55)

Because these approaches acknowledge the musical component of listening and composing, they are (as I find) deeply engaging, intuitive and satisfying. They do, however, defer to subjectivity by invoking a more relative rather than absolute concept of 'level' than lower-level mapping strategies. Approaches can, of course, be mixed: an oceanic wave melody can be quantized to a mode whose brightness is determined by the lunar cycle, and yet both mappings remain entirely systematic; some pixelation notwithstanding, the data can be both reconstructed and felt.

Let us return to our heartbeat. As we travel further to the right on the analogic-symbolic continuum, levels of information and continuity are sacrificed in exchange for the 'discrete' in the data. For example, by focusing only on the distance between the R peaks – determined by surpassing a threshold in level of electrical activity, or an up-down spike – then our data stream becomes either a measure of pulse rate rather than pulse shape. This RR interval (or, inversely, pulse rate or BPM) can in itself be mapped to any sonic parameter, to create a pulse-rate melody (Figure 4h), brightness contour, or similar. It is true that we have now lost information between these peaks, but this focus on pulse rate may benefit both information conveyance and effective musical translation. The pulses could trigger audio samples or dictate the tempo of a pre-existing (or live-generated) passage of music. This 'reMapping' technique (Gresham-Lancaster & Sinclair, 2012) is illustrated in Figure 4f. While a focus on BPM alone is lossy, we can dial back the level of abstraction to recover some nuance in the heart-rate contour. By lowering our threshold and listening out for the T peaks, we now have an RTR intervallic pattern, suitable for mapping onto a swing rhythm of various time-feels (Mermikides, 2010:89–91).

We can push far into the discrete and symbolic end of the continuum while maintaining useful informational and musical communication. Among the most discrete and symbolic representations is perhaps an auditory icon alerting us that some target BPM has been reached (Figure 4j). So long as it indicates this discrete event effectively, the sound itself need not have any direct connection to the data. Still such icons allow some sophistication, some logical syntax, such as two clarinet notes marking the second consecutive minute of elevated heart rate or three double bass notes for the third consecutive minute of low heart rate. In summary, even the simplest data stream has endless systematic translation systems, each drawing focus to and revealing particular properties of the data. This can be done by inscribing the data directly into the sonic signal or by having the data instruct simple abstract sonic symbols – or any complex interweaving and intersectional approaches between these extremes.

2.4 Temporalities

Sound is temporal, and music is a temporal art. They unfold in time, and their experience is intrinsically bound to that temporal ribbon. Time (and its measures of duration and frequency) make up the fundamental fabric of music: a passage of sound material exists as – and can be transformed between – the pitch spectrum and a number of overlapping rhythmic strata, where pitch and rhythm are connected but experientially distinct domains. The rhythm domain is a primary vehicle in music psychology – the BRECVEMA model, for example, dedicates two of its eight expressive mechanisms to the time-based components of musical expectancy and rhythmic entrainment (see Juslin, 2013). Extreme time manipulations can convert a dissonant chord to a slow complex polyrhythm, while the subtlest deviations from the rhythmic grid can produce deep expressivity. While it takes time (from a short glance to an extended perusal) to absorb a piece of visual art, a passage of music takes as long as it takes and is either listened to in its entirety or abandoned. This is not to say that all music is conceived or delivered as a linear strip. Examples of nonlinear structures abound in both practice and theory, from simple repeat signs, open vamps to endless beat circles – as in the disarmingly neat presentations of flamenco rhythmic *compás* as points on a clock face. Retrograde and palindromic manipulations of rhythmic and motivic material – through notation and technology – are also well established. Still other approaches are non-linear, drawing temporally free selections from a library of musical materials, be it an internal knowledge base, cells in notation or MIDI and audio clips. A non-linear approach is even obligatory in some practices, such as the live scoring demanded in some video game music, and other sound practices that allow the listener to interact with an indeterminate strip of time. However it is used, time makes up the material of music; its impact can rely equally on short-term memory or distant nostalgia. The musical experience involves a complex interplay between the sounding objects, which are external to the listener, and subjective and internal 'virtual reference structures' (Danielsen, 2010:6), which turn a continuous flow of information into layers of predictive nodes (or waves). In short, music is entirely dependent on time to function, but in the process, music transforms our experience of time. And yet despite these manipulations and the rich and complex temporal experiences they produce, music and sound are ultimately received as a singular waveform (or two, given the usual number of ears per listener). While pitch is often conceived in the vertical dimension, timbre as colour or texture, and rhythm as grids and circles, the ultimate (and only) delivery system is on a fixed conveyor belt of time. Music may well be multidimensional, but one dimension is hard-wired to time. This is very useful to bear in mind when representing data in the sonic domain, where we essentially have multiple temporal representations to coordinate and curate.

In the sonification process, a data set may include a time component (EEG, ECG, oceanic waves, birth rates, orbital periods and so on), it is then a natural (but not necessary) choice to carry over that time domain allocation into the sonic realm: When an event – or parameter value – occurs in the data, there is a synchronised event – or change – in the sonic domain. This might happen at the same rate as the data – such as a parameter mapping of a heartbeat or oceanic wave – or the data set can be scaled to be made audible – or to be heard with a different aural filter – in the pitch or rhythmic spectrum. In a sense, some data is merely transposed (perhaps with a systematic – say logarithmic – transformation) from one portion of the temporal spectrum to another.[23] This can be done with a high level of abstraction, as in my composition *Slow Light* (3.1.9), where red

---

[23] Images from space often use a similar transposition of light information into the visible spectrum. The structures exist, but are only made visible to our relative narrow range of vision, through this frequency shift.

light waves translate to low pitches and blue light to higher pitches. The translation from light wave to sound wave frequency is not strict, but in both domains, there is an appropriate spectral ordering in between the slow and fast wave forms.

We can even choose to take a data component and create a one-to-many mapping to the time dimension, as in *Distant Harmony* (Section 3.1.6), where the repeating orbital periodicity of each planet of the Solar System is scaled to the pitch and rhythm domain simultaneously – an approach I call a bonded melorhythm. By speeding its orbit to both the pitch and rhythmic domains, Mercury emits a rapidly repeating high pulse, while Saturn's pulse is slow and low. The same data is thus reinforced by two simultaneous mappings in the temporal domain. Other data sets may not include a strictly temporal component – think of a skyline, a string of text or a genomic sequence – but can be read, scanned or scrubbed through: an implied ordering binds the spatial dimension to the time dimension. We can, for example, trace the population of a country along a line of longitude: the temporal dimension in the sonic realm is now a measure, not of time, but of geographical position. Even if a data set does have a time component, we are not obliged to represent it as time in the sonification – temporal distances can be rerouted to a different parameter, freeing the time dimension in the sonification for a different use. For example, Figure 4d represents a portion of the heartbeat contour as an evolving chord in which pitches represent temporal distance and the fading in and out of those pitches – over time – represents electrical activity. A slower heart rate would produce a wider-spaced chord, and its contour would dictate how this voicing changed in the (sonic) time domain. Such a use of 'inverted' time is employed in *Primal Sound* (Section 3.1.1)

Even if a data set has no time implication (or if we choose to discard it) the time dimension in the sonification is still available to us; however brief or cyclical, it is inescapable. We can use this built-in time-dimension in music for whatever parameter we like: indeed, a data set that lacks any time dimension or clear sense of spatial or logical ordering *obligates* the sonifier to make temporal decisions, whether derived from the data or otherwise. Suppose, for example, that we have a single blood pressure reading with measures for systolic and diastolic pressure. These two values – if abstracted from their original locations in the time dimension – might be presented in the pitch domain as a two-note chord (with higher pitch representing higher pressure) or as a cross rhythm, with each pressure reading controlling a low-frequency oscillator (LFO). The duration of this presentation is up to us: while it should be long enough for the message to be absorbed, there is nothing in the data to dictate how long we hear its sonification. In the case of the pitch translation the data has been presented almost immediately, in the rhythm we might (but are not obliged to) let the phased rhythm wrap-around. Either way, our sonification uses a cyclical fragment of time, and it is up to us – as curators of the data – how to present it to the listener.

In sonifying material, we must deal with temporality at various stages in the process. First, we identify temporality in the data set and consider if the data possesses an inherent time, spatial or ordering dimension that we wish to carry over into the sonification. We then deal with temporality in the mapping process and consider how the data is to be represented in the pitch and rhythmic domain (analogously or symbolically). This mapping can be simple, with one periodicity or contour mapped into one time domain, or it can form a complex web of temporal mappings. Finally, we address temporality in the presentation of the sonification itself. If the data is from a linear process – an exploding star, say, or the use of a parking space over a single day – the experience for the listener may be a simple one-to-one representation (scaled or not). If the data – or its sonification – lack any time component corresponding to real-world clock time, we are again left with the decision of curating it for the listener. In any case, we might play the sonification once, or we might repeat it in its entirety (as Villa-Lobos does with his skyline), or indefinitely. We might take fragments of the sonified material and replay them at different rates, like a telescope zooming into the data. We might even give control over to a live performer or listener, providing an interactive sonic graph (see Figure 4e) to be explored at will. In every instance, there are three opportunities to engage with temporality: in the data set, in the mapping and in the final presentation. At each stage, the sonifier is responsible for considering how best to communicate the data to the listener.

2.5 Tools and the Canvas

2.5.1 Tools and Technologies

Some of the techniques so far discussed are accessible to all composers through manual notation or a digital audio workstation (DAW), duly carrying material from the data to the sonic realm. Certainly, a cryptogram or skyline might require nothing more than paper and pencil. However, depending on the size of the data set and complexity of the chosen technique, translation may require a significant investment of time. Unlike notation, the DAW offers helpful, if not essential, technological assistance, allowing as it does off-grid temporal flexibility, visual markers and more intuitive data editing. Still the process of using a DAW can be extraordinarily intensive, as well as subject to error and datablindness. Not that it is always unpleasant: In my earlier sonification projects I spent many hours in such activities, slipping into a near meditative state as I stared at each video frame of a parking space or flap of a bird's wing, sliding in auditory icons to the nearest 40 ms, and only breaking focus to shake my head at the absurdity and strange beauty of the task. Even for a composer willing to undertake such projects, the absence of any technological automation in the translation process discourages experimentation with different systems and data sets, while its presence encourages one to repeat and finesse a given system. Without automation, certain methods become impractical or impossible, including audification, continuous mapping and real-time sonifications. With it, some processes become possible, others more practical and efficient; but technology also supports a level of objectivity and systematic approach in the craft, preserving the rule-base – and aiding the repeatability – of Hermann's criteria.

Whether it is used to calculate simple functions or to generate complex sounds, there is almost no stage in the sonification process where technology cannot be co-opted: from the beginning of the process to the end, these include **data collection and preparation** (collating and appropriately presenting the data set), **data translation** (the systematic translation of the data set to the sonic domain materials), **sonic material generation** (the mapping or bonding of sonic data and instructions to human and machine instruments), **modelling** (technological simulation of data abstractions) and **production** (curating, presenting and displaying the material in the audio and acoustic domains). Some projects might incorporate technological automation into only some of these stages, while others might fuse together various stages into a highly automated – even real-time – process. For example, my project *Distant Harmony* (Section 3.1.6) began with a simple Excel sheet where the orbital periods of each planet are manually entered, and column calculations automatically translated these to values in both the rhythmic and audio domains. For the first exhibition, these were manually configured into the DAW, tuning and adjusting the pulse of software instruments accordingly. A more sophisticated system might generate the pulses automatically from the input data, but with just eight planets, two other similar-sized planetary systems and an impending deadline, this approach was sensible enough. Projects which sonify processes captured on video might use the DAW as a helpful visual scanner, entering MIDI notes frame by frame, creating a network of timed identified events, then using the flexibility of MIDI to experiment with a range of mappings and translation rules (see *Another Day*, Section 3.1.8). Tools are also available to read visual data and output MIDI or audio material automatically, such as my *Kandinsky* tool, which keeps a digital eye on specified pixels of an image or video file. These readers can be fixated on just one spot of a video, reporting activity and colour data and generating corresponding analogic and symbolic mappings into the sonic realm, all in real time. Max for Live – the integration of Cycling 74's Max/MSP into the Ableton Live environment – provides real-time and readily configurable live data streams within a familiar DAW environment.

Asteroid, climate, cryptographic, traffic and other live-input data can generate MIDI (which can then be further modified with other devices) to virtual instruments. Mappings can be made, disconnected, scaled and moved on the fly, all within a familiar and recallable metric framework and audio network.

Some of these approaches might seem daunting to a composer, who wonders how they can possibly find, build or use such esoteric devices in their practice. Ironically, many of us happily use technological devices from laptops to mobiles to Wi-Fi to MIDI keyboards to RAM to SSD drives to microwave ovens with minimal, if any, understanding of their inner mechanics. We care *that* they work (or not), how they are operated and that they obey instructions as expected, but we are not troubled by the deeper *how*. When it comes to sonification devices, however, composers can lose this naive relationship with technology and become overwhelmed with the responsibility for these inner processes, feeling an apparent need to understand the mechanics beneath the surface.

In fact, knowing the right questions to ask is halfway to the solution. Say we were inspired by Villa-Lobos and wanted to convert an image of a skyline to a melody using a programming language like Max/MSP. We should ask a series of questions such as: Is it possible to load an image so that its internal data can be accessed? (Yes – a Jitter matrix.) We want to read it from left to right, so Is there a way to take just one vertical slice of this matrix and move it in relation to some master clock? (Yes – *jit.submatrix* takes one vertical slice; *transport* moves it.) What counts as a skyline? Is there a way to find an edge – do we need to prepare the images beforehand? Is there a way to output the vertical position of the edge, relative to a baseline? Can we convert this spatial position to the position of a pitch within a range? Can the resulting set of pitches be quantized to any divisions of the octave, or to a scale? In a horizontal section of the skyline, should the note repeat or be sustained? Is velocity (dynamics) addressed in any way in the translation? These are the sort of fundamental questions in any sonification process, and all the answers to them are usually answerable. Finding out exactly how to address such questions may take minutes, hours or days of research – perhaps with external assistance – and some approaches may need to be rethought for practical or technical reasons. Nevertheless, asking the right questions – avoiding the trap of scrutinising every device's internal library – is the central skill in dealing with technology, one that can be surprisingly simple, engaging and rewarding.

2.5.2 The Scope and Colour of the Canvas

It is an attractive notion to consider a sonification to be the *sound of* or even *the music of* the domain under study, be it brain activity, tidal patterns, a black hole or molecular processes. While the magic – and even the purpose – of the sonification may be connected to the idea of revealing music within data, we should maintain a sober and lucid view on the process. Some forms of audification, it is true, might be considered *the sound of* the data – that is to say, what we would hear if only we were capable of hearing a wider range of dynamics and frequencies. But if our sonification utilises any level of symbolic representation, then we are using sound (and music) as a metaphorical language through which to understand and intuitively absorb data relations and patterns. In this sense, the music is comparable to a visual graph, which neither is nor looks like its domain, but which provides an understanding of patterns within it. In my own sonification activity, I aim for there to be both a fair and objective representation of the data, and for salient patterns and relationships in the domain to be heard, appreciated and *felt*. Rather than sounding out the data directly, we are making a sonic canvas upon which patterns in the data can be projected. This canvas – the nexus of sonic objects and transformations under the command of the data – is rarely, if ever, *neutral*. We must choose a duration, an ensemble of 'carrier' instruments, smooth or variously striated partitions of time and pitch, textural, harmonic and dynamic contexts and so on. Imagine reverberated choral voices with soft transients and slow-changing harmonies; or insistent melodic cells on panned marimbas syncopated, phased and rotated by the data; or wide cut-off frequencies and resonance shaping of a metronomic square-wave synth ostinato: representing the same data, each would contribute significantly to the nature of the sonic experience, and its aesthetic and emotive connotations – choral, minimalist and electronic dance music, respectively. Even an attempt at emotional neutrality and avoidance of stylistic tropes – say with non-committal [025] pitch-class sets, sine waves, mechanical velocities – rapidly becomes a style-by-omission. In short, we can't avoid making some degree of sonic – and ultimately musical – decisions, however objective our data representation.

In these regards there are two fundamental questions to ask of any sonification system: (a) How sensitive and varied is the sonic output in response to different data? And (b) To what extent does the canvas colour the sonic output, regardless of the data? The answer to (a) is genuinely much narrower, and (b) more extensive than many care to admit, but they are still questions worth addressing. Most translation systems can be improved by calibrating both the range of input data and resulting sonic output, making them more sensitive to changes within and between data sets. In addition, the canvas can be crafted so that it presents – rather *bleeding through* and masking – variations in data. With such considerations, Hermann's principle of *recognisability* is better addressed, and the sonification might remain objective, recognisable, accessible and even musically transporting.

3 The Sonification Experience

3.1 Example Projects

This section presents brief overviews of some sonification projects (2004–2023) which have been selected to illustrate the wide range of data domains, techniques and approaches available to the contemporary composer. Dates are given for first public output, but many of the projects are ongoing, with resources and concepts shared and developed between pieces. The narrative for each project also includes a discussion of its *afterlife*: how the project was received, how it developed, how it resonated with different audiences, and what further projects it inspired – each speaking to how insight and impact, for me and others, may emerge beyond the sonic object in itself. Projects are presented here as succinctly as possible; audio-visual materials and technical details are available on the book's companion website.

3.1.1 Primal Sound (2004)

Artist & sculptor Angela Palmer has received much acclaim for her science-art crossover works. These include MRI images of an Egyptian mummy, a public exhibition of felled Amazonian trees in Trafalgar Square and a photography exhibit of the most, and least, polluted places on earth (Palmer, 2023). In January 2004, she approached me with a particular project in mind. She had recently encountered the following passage in Rainer Maria Rilke's *Ur-Geräusch* (Primal Sound) and found in it an irresistible challenge:

> *The coronal suture of the skull (which should now be chiefly investigated) has let us assume a certain similarity to the closely wound line that the needle of a phonograph cuts into the receptive, revolving cylinder of the machine. Suppose, for instance, one played a trick on this needle and caused it to retrace a path not made by the graphic translation of a sound, but self-sufficing and existing in nature – good, let us say it boldly, if it were (e.g.) even the coronal suture – what would happen? A sound must come into being, a sequence of sounds, music ... Feelings of what sort? Incredulity, awe, fear, reverence yes, which of all these feelings prevents me from proposing a name for the primal sound that would then come to birth?* (Rilke, 1919:1087)

Palmer hoped to commission a piece of music inspired by this text, to be used in a gallery exhibition alongside the skull of an unknown Victorian woman, contemporaneous with Rilke.

Rilke's essay is in effect calling for audification, and so a digital tracing of an image of the skull was translated into sound, producing a short but visceral tear in the audio domain. With the resources available, this simple 'phonographic' rendering of the contour did not provide enough material for a piece of any significant length (and some loopbacks in the contour were unmappable). The solution was to map its shape to a variety of parameters – as if simultaneously rendering some of the options in Figure 4 – so that it dictates all the sonic output in an example of *isokinetos* ('equal or fixed gesture").[24] In addition to the initial phonographic rendering, the contour is rendered as a microtonal melody. Then, as a harmonic backdrop, a just-intonated scale (A Lydian in Pythagorean temperament) is mapped against the vertical orientation of the contour (in a manner similar to Figure 4d). Finally, a slow translation introduces single sine-wave tones that split as the loops of the contour curve away, creating a gradually converging and diverging harmonic texture. The resulting beating frequencies become a recurrent motif in the piece.

Musical events in *Primal Sound* are created – and also organised structurally – according to systems guided by the coronal suture itself.[25] New events (microtonal melody, audification, etc.) are triggered by each looping point of the contour. The pan position of the triggered event is determined by the vertical position of the loop point, moving through the stereo field until it is faded slowly after crossing the central line. Since, on occasion, adjacent loops occur on the same side of the central line, multiple musical events may coexist.

Primal Sound was commissioned initially for an art installation piece (running for five months continuously at a single exhibition at the Royal College of Surgeons): thus, its 'loopability' needed to be considered. The compositional structure was determined by following the coronal suture over the top of the skull before looping back around the inside to end at the starting point for the next repetition of the piece.

That such rich material could emerge on a relatively empty canvas[26] from the audification and parameter mapping of a single contour was quite a transformative experience; it was as though the piece was plucked from thin air. However, despite its specificity, *Primal Sound* has been used in contexts divorced from its origin – most notably in the soundtrack to the documentary *Martino Unstrung* as a representation of Martino's geometric musical vision.

---

[24] See Mermikides (2010:56–68) for a categorisation of improvisations or compositions in terms of fixing (prefix *iso-*) or varying (prefix *dis-*) a variety of musical parameters, such as metric position (placement), timbre, gestural shape (*kinetos*), intensity (*paesi*), rhythmic figure, melodic pitch set, etc. Novel strategies such as isomelos, distrimbe and isokinetos are formulated among the familiar ones of isorhythm, displacement etc.

[25] For an in-depth discussion of the relationship between Rilke's vision and my piece, see Huss (2024).

[26] The most colouring aspect of the translation is the choice of scale for the harmonic backdrop. Quantizing to a scale of a particular dreamy quality narrows the range that other contours would produce. I have since adapted this contour approach (e.g. for coastlines) so that the pattern of the contour – through its shape and relative distance of loops – determines the scale (and thus canvas).

3.1.2 Bloodlines (2004–)

While undergoing treatment for leukaemia in an isolation ward at Charing Cross Hospital in 2004–2005, I underwent daily tests for a range of blood cell types. These were monitored closely for signs of infection, relapse and immunity level. This close inspection revealed patterns of population growth, and the idea of mapping these to a musical composition soon suggested itself. *Primal Sound* uses just one contour to create multiple musical layers, but the fourteen blood cell types in *Bloodlines* allow for a parallel approach, with each contour controlling just one of the fourteen simultaneous musical layers.

These melodic voices are derived in a variety of ways, from fairly simple microtonal glide (white blood cells) and MIDI pitch translations of values (platelets) to more complex mappings. For example, haematocrit (HCT) testing of red blood cells was provided in the form of four-digit numbers, each digit calling up one of ten samples (0–9) for each semiquaver subdivision of a beat. This latter translation is the most symbolic of the blood cells, and may not pass the criteria of relevance, but it does convey change and activity. The other blood cells indicate clearly the unfolding narrative of the disease.

Each day of treatment is translated into one second of music, and the undulations in health can be heard musically as the piece progresses. In particular, the prominent microtonal swell can be heard to descend as the white blood cell count starts extremely high due to the leukaemic cells, and is massively reduced by chemotherapy until the body reaches a vulnerable neutropaenia (0:30–0:40). The 'autobiological' nature of the work engenders an emotive response and memory of the journey through treatment, and I recognise each day of treatment in each second of the music.

Bloodlines has been disseminated at conferences, used in exhibitions and broadcast in an interview on BBC Radio 4's Midweek (BBC, 2015). Later it became the foundation of a hybrid lecture-theatre piece by my sister – and bone marrow donor – Alex Mermikides. This was performed internationally (with a fully sonified score) and alongside a catalyst project *Careful* (which turned the empathetic gaze from patient to nurse) used as training material for medical students and professionals (see Mermikides, A. 2021:87–117).

3.1.3 Microcosmos (2007)

A 2007 Wellcome Trust grant provided the opportunity to explore yet more complex hidden musical concepts in a large-scale work, now in collaboration with scientists. Microcosmos is an audio/video installation that presents high-quality images of bacterial colonies shot by photographer Steve Downer, whose work also includes BBC's *Blue Planet*, *Life on Earth* and *Planet Earth*, all set to a 4.1 surround sonified soundtrack. Simon Park, a professor of microbiology at the University of Surrey, provided scientific insight and supervision of the microbacterial colonies. The aims of the project were several, but as a sonifier I was confronted with one problem in particular: how to work with both video footage and biological data? The final compositional system would have to create a satisfying sound design from overt visual aspects of the video material: colour and form. It would also have to incorporate a systematic way of responding to portions of each microbacteria's DNA sequences, so that each colony had its own recognizable sound.

Rather than impose an anthropocentric 'emotional' film score on the video footage, there was an intention to design a system that would respond automatically to video and biological data in a way that was at once aesthetically satisfying, complex and not distractingly predictable. The sound design aimed to mirror aspects of the growth of microbacterial colonies: emergent large-scale structures from the interactive behaviour of simple components.

The electronic system designed for the work became absolutely integral and indispensable to the sound design (the interactions being far too complex to be undertaken manually). Once constructed, it allowed a virtually 'hands-off' compositional process. However, unlike *Bloodlines* – where physical parameters controlled coexisting yet independently generated musical layers – *Microcosmos* constructs a complex interrelationship between variables. This interdependence of parameters does not set up a simple one-to-one response between one particular input value and one isolated musical event. Small changes in one colour can pass a tipping point and trigger a series of non-linear events in a way that – despite the systematic translation process – feels improvisational, reactive and unpredictable.[27]

The core of the compositional system is dependent on patches written in Cycling '74's MAX/MSP 4.5 and Jitter 1.6 (*What's The Point?* and *Gene Genie*). Ableton Live 6 was also used in synchronisation with Max/MSP for audio synthesis and manipulation. Recording, editing and mastering was conducted with Logic Pro 7, an Audient Mixing Console and an M&K 5.1 monitoring system.

The first exhibition of this installation (at the Guildford International Music Festival in 2007) used a Samsung 52" plasma screen, four Eclipse TD monitors and an Eclipse sub-bass speaker. Subsequent exhibitions, in Antwerp and various parts of England, took the form of large-scale projections.

---

[27] Full technical details on the translation process are available in Mermikides (2010: 'Practice':18–28).

Several of the DNA translation concepts were brought forward to later projects, including the Genomusicology (Section 3.1.12) series. Meanwhile viruses and bacteria continue to fascinate me, leading to such works as *Musical Culture* (2017). This was a collaboration with Konstanze Hild (teaching fellow at the University of Surrey's Advanced Technology Institute), who researches microbacteria and their resistance to antibiotics. Here the growth rates of bacteria in response to antibiotic exposure are translated into pitch classes over time. The contrapuntal shifts and additions of lines create surprising but logical harmonic shifts, from which I have taken inspiration for conventional (that is, somewhat less bacterial) composition.

3.1.4 Geometudes (2014–)

Geometudes is an ongoing series of sonifications of geometric and mathematical processes. Hundreds of outputs have now been produced (and enabled through bespoke technology), but the project began with a small set of pieces, *Geometudes 1–5*. The name is both a contraction of 'geometrical etudes' and a nod to Erik Satie's *Gymnopédies*. Each sonification is created by the intersection of geometrical shapes (lines and various polygons), with pitches assigned to their corners and vertices. As the shapes pass through each other, the pitches are sounded. Conventional music notation essentially treats pitch and durational structures as being carried on a flat conveyor belt and pulled through a static temporal point (or 'playhead'), where they are sounded. Here, however, time has a more abstracted and complex function. The rotation, velocity, gravity and trajectory of these shapes produce a range of motivic transformations well beyond the conventional use of retrograde, inversion and geometrical expansion and contraction. At times, deeply expressive moments are heard and surprising motivic characters are created, despite their systematic and limited origins. In *Geometude I: Triangle and Line*, a drifting triangle loaded with three notes, produces not just every ordering of the three-note set, with two notes sometimes sounding at once, but also a fluid set of relative durations. In *Geometude III*, the low-gravity spin of a hexagon – loaded with a Satie hexachord – produces disarmingly expressive rhythmic inflections, as the objects drift through each other in countless ways. *Geometude V* is a lullaby for four rotating polygons and an attempt to send my then two-year-old daughter to sleep.[28] Such geometric transformations have now entered my broad compositional and teaching practice, and I have recently turned to the challenge of notating them for human players.

---

[28] It didn't work.

More ambitious pieces in the Geometudes series have their own titles. *Irrational Music* (2015) was created as a (good-natured, I think) response to a critic who declared my music overly repetitive. Here the digits (0–9) of successive decimal places of ε, φ and π are symbolically linked to ten musical objects, which are sent in turn to three instruments playing in a hocketed triple time.[29] The resulting music may sound minimalistic but is provably not repetitive. If played for an infinite duration, any imaginable sequence of these objects, however long, is bound to exist at some point. *Geometudes I–V* and *Irrational Music* were animated for exhibitions by long-time collaborator Anna Tanczos of SciComm Studios.

Pendulum Music is a direct sonification of a video recording of fifteen uncoupled simple pendulums, built by Nils Sorensen of Harvard Natural Sciences Lecture Demonstrations (Sorensen, 2010); Sorensen also produced the video. The changing string lengths and oscillation periods produce a mesmerising range of travelling, standing and beating waves. Each pendulum is mapped to trigger an individual note at its apex, collectively producing three octaves of a just-intonated Japanese *Yo* scale. The resulting motifs and emergent patterns are as engaging sonically as they are visually and seem to defy the putative limitations of a pentatonic scale. This sonic experiment felt too musically useful to leave alone, and I have since built a device, *Arpendulus*, which produces MIDI arpeggiations based on virtual pendula with changeable (and mappable) string lengths, bob weights, gravity, string tension and friction. I have employed such devices among the artillery of familiar audio and MIDI processors for commercial music appearing on Netflix, Disney and the Discovery Channel, completely divorced from any sonification framing. This translation from observed to abstracted data processes is an example of 'naturally-sourced' algorithmic music (see lower left of Figure 1), and there is an abundance of such processes available to the curious composer.

3.1.5 Sound Asleep (2014–)

Sound Asleep is a project series made in collaboration with sleep scientists Debra Skene (University of Surrey), Morten Kringelbach (University of Oxford), Vladyslav Vyazovskiy (University of Oxford), Renata Riha (University of Edinburgh) and several sleep researchers, video, audio and computer programmers. The project develops techniques that allow the systematic translation of sleep data into sound, with a number of outputs and events based on these systems. Through sonification, such phenomena as the disruption of sleep in

---

[29] Octave displacements occur when digits are repeated, but the translation is completely isomorphic.

the visually impaired, sleep apnoea and the transitions in brainwave activity between sleep states are captured and translated, allowing a musical communication – and visceral appreciation – of this information. The project has been disseminated to members of diverse communities – sleep science, visually impaired, sleep disorder, music and wider – allowing us all to experience this otherwise hidden – yet vital – part of our lives.

Sleep research produces a wide range of data and thus opportunities for rich and diverse sonification opportunities. Here is a sample:

Nocturnes – in collaboration with Renata Riha and Anna Tanczos (video) – employs an entirely systematic translation system to convert polysomnographic data (PSG) into a virtual score. A flute melody dictated by sleep state (descending when falling asleep, trilling on REM and silent when awake), strings and harp by oxygen transfer (SPO2), breathing interruptions (apnoea), periodic leg movements (PLM) and snoring by pizzicato and percussion, and body position by a bass line. In *Nocturne I: Deep Sleep*, the subject's enviably good night's sleep produces a correspondingly peaceful musical output, with a cinematic tranquil diatonicism. *Nocturne II: Breathless* employs exactly the same translation system as *Nocturne I*, but the subject – who has severe apnoea – creates a starkly different soundworld. The orchestration reveals how apnoea and body-movement events coordinate with the fitful sleep episodes. In *Nocturne III: Restless*, the same translation system is applied to a subject with restless leg syndrome, producing constant movement in bass line and percussion, and a frustrated sleep flute melody that never resolves. The harp glissando at the beginning occurs when the subject remembers to attach their SpO2 sensor.

In *Inner Sound of Sleep*, electroencephalographic (EEG) data of a subject during sleep (provided by Vyazovskiy) is translated using audification and parameter mapping. The sonification is presented in real time to an accompanying visualisation by Tanczos, with several extracts through the night sampled. A prominent frequency can be heard falling in pitch with deeper sleep states, and rising rapidly during REM state associated with dreaming.

Sleep Maps is a series of sonifications, based on collaborator Skene's work on the circadian rhythm ('body clock') and its relationship with light exposure and melatonin exposure (see, e.g. Potter et al., 2016). *49:48* presents the phasing mismatch between the 24-hour clock and the typical circadian body clock of 24.5 hours. In the absence of regulating melatonin and light cues, the resulting 49:48 polyrhythm produces a slow but persistent phase, revealing our tendency – in the absence of light signals – to stay up a little later each night. Melodic material is superimposed upon itself at this ratio, creating a slow expressive phasing, with each day represented by a modal shift. Additional *Sleep Maps* sonify the melatonin peak, night-time sleep and day-time napping of subjects with a variety of sleep disorders and visual impairments, revealing a wide range of phasing and rhythmic patterns.

Transitions is a project initiated by Kringelbach, whose research reveals that a human's passage from wakefulness to sleep involves – rather than a simple trajectory – a complex web of interlinking states, nineteen of which have been identified (see Stevner et al., 2019). Some can be traversed in both directions, while others are one-way: some paths are more likely than others, overall providing multiple routes (and dead ends) from full wakefulness to deep sleep. The resulting map is staggeringly similar to harmonic flowcharts found in analytical and compositional models (see, for example, Lehman, 2013). This latent structure provides not just one sonic output but a source of many possible musical solutions. The pathway structure, groups and nineteen nodes fit elegantly with the nineteen trichords of pitch-class set theory, and as such is a suitable site for functional harmonic cadences. But the approach that proved to be most communicative employs the hidden Markov mode as a Neo-Riemannian harmonic map, which yields both familiar and surprising voice-leading transformations. It offers – and employs built-in programming to produce – not just the surface translation of a singular sleep experience, but an underlying blueprint to create countless trajectories for the multitudes of possible sleep.

The *Sound Asleep* project has been presented as keynotes at the British Sleep Society conference at the Sage Gateshead in October 2015, Royal Physiological Society in December 2018, and Royal Society of Medicine in February 2020. In 2019, *Sound Asleep* works were exhibited at the Design Museum, London, and featured on BBC Radio 4's *Inside Science*. In February 2020, BBC Radio Scotland used Sound Asleep outputs to reveal the sleep patterns of visually impaired participants to the presenter Ian Hamilton, a disability activist who is himself visually impaired.

3.1.6 Distant Harmony (2015–)

Distant Harmony is an ongoing series of projects derived from astronomical data. Music has always been associated with movements of the planets – think of Pythagoras's harmony of the spheres or Kepler's planetary scales[30] – but these projects add a contemporary fidelity, both in the use of highly accurate NASA data (in consultation with space scientist Rob Scott) and in the microtonal and micro-temporal sonic output.

Distant Harmony I–III employ 'bonded melorhythms': that is to say, the orbital periods of planetary systems are repeatedly sped up by powers of two

---

[30] See Kepler's 1619 *Harmonice Mundi*, Kepler et al., 1997.

(octave transpositions) until they enter the (1) rhythmic and (2) pitch domains of human perception, producing both a polyrhythm and a harmony; they are then rendered electronically to millisecond and cent (1/100th semitone) accuracy. This results in microrhythmic and microtonal material, unbounded by common musical conventions. *Distant Harmony* has been broadcast and discussed on Radio 4's *Rhythm of Life* series, hosted by Evelyn Glennie (Glennie, 2018), the New Scientist Podcast (New Scientist, 2021) and employed in several international conferences and exhibitions, with video animations by Anna Tanczos.

In *Distant Harmony I* (2015), the orbital frequencies of the Solar System's planets are translated into rhythms (24 octaves up) and pitches (35 octaves up). The audible pitch range is not quite wide enough to allow a uniform transposition, so Uranus and Neptune are transposed up by a couple of octaves, but their relative ordering and micro pitch class are systematic. Although pitch and rhythm are analogic, each planet is given a symbolic timbral identity. Despite the microtonal pitch system and microphasing, the resulting melorhythm is surprisingly consonant, revealing a harmonic resonance. In the video animation, the orbital periods are presented as independent and circular (rather than elliptical) for visual clarity. On the suggestion of a visually impaired attendee at the 2021 Astrosonification Conference at the University of Groningen, an alternate version includes speech sonically labelling each planet.

Distant Harmony II (2015) is a bonded melorhythmic translation of the planetary orbits of 55 Cancri, a binary star system about 41 light-years away. The planet 55 Cancri E (the first to appear in the animation) is thought to have a third of its mass made up of diamonds, with a value of about £18 quintillion.

Distant Harmony III HD10180 (2015) is a bonded melorhythmic translation of HD10180, which is the largest known exoplanetary system, similar to our solar system in its planets' sizes. Orbital periods are transposed up by 24 and 33 octaves respectively. In these first three Distant Harmony works, the melorhythms of each systems can be sonically distinguished. With over five thousand exoplanetary systems already discovered – and billions yet to be – we are unlikely to run out of data for new works any time soon.

Distant Harmony IV – StarStuff (2015) is perhaps the simplest sonification discussed in this book. It is just a representation of the rate of star birth in the universe (4,800 stars are born each second).[31] This is so fast that – if sounded – it would be perceived as pitch, not rhythm. The piece is a single sustained sine wave at 4.8 kHz (about four octaves and a second above middle C) which in exhibition is played over a short text explanation.

---

[31] Recent estimates put this closer to 3,300 a second, and I have updated the piece accordingly.

3.1.7 Crystals, Rocks and Minerals (2015–)

In 2015, microbiologist Simon Park (University of Surrey) produced a series of high-quality videos depicting the formation of salt crystals. *Crystals* (2015) maps this highly engaging process to a virtual piano keyboard, with growth on the left and right of the screen systematically translated into low and high notes respectively. The height on the screen is (inversely) translated to note velocity. *Dark Shards* (2015) employs a similar translation system to *Crystals*, and in this case the particular crystallising choreography produces a more angular motivic language.

These pieces have been presented at several exhibitions and events, and among other *Hidden Music* works were featured on the New Scientist Podcast (New Scientist, 2021). The hosts were generously enthusiastic about the sonifications, noting its semblance to 'legitimate music', and articulating quite succinctly some of this book's intended messages:

> That's kind of the joy of it, you can make it as complex or as simple as you want... What I think is really valuable about data sonification is that not only can you create something really beautiful and interesting, as we've just heard, it's a really simple way of conveying a lot of complex information at once, in a way that people who aren't necessarily experts can engage with. Our ears are really sensitive to the variations that we hear in sound so you don't need a lot of scientific or even musical training to spot those patterns, and only using visual representations of data can exclude a lot of blind and visually impaired people as well. So sonification just provides another route into engaging with the data. (Ackerley in New Scientist, 2021)

A project is underway – *Rock Music* – to sonify the geological strata of the Grand Canyon from bottom to top, sounding out its 1.84-billion-year geological history.

3.1.8 Music of People and Other Animals (2015–)

While humans are usually the active – and only – creators of music, I have long been interested in the generation of music from the unconscious behaviour of humans. Where we choose to sit in a train carriage, our navigation through a party, our predictably irrational purchasing decisions (Kahneman, 2011), all such behaviours are patterns of interest and illumination. Here follow some projects exploring such data in the behaviour of humans and other animals.

Another Day (2015) is created by converting a 24-hour period of an entire road's bus stops, lighting system and parking spaces to notes distributed among the instruments of a virtual orchestra (e.g. horns, percussion, strings on left, middle, right respectively). Loading bays and illegal parking are assigned more dissonant and percussive material, which become more frenetic during rush hour. The spaces are always active, even when a careless unwitting performer spills a bucket of water over a loading zone. Video: Anna Tanczos.

Birth & Death (2015) is a real-time simulation of global birth and death rates (in right-hand and left-hand parts respectively). The areas of the keyboard are assigned to continents. The approximate 11:5 polyrhythm ensures an unrelenting global population growth.

Groningen Harp (2016). During my residency at the Frank Mohr Institute, I was granted access and permission to Groningen's CCTV on a main vantage point. This allowed the entire city to become an unwitting orchestra. In one example, the lines on the road become a harp, with highly complex polyrhythms emerging from varying walking and cycling speeds.

Web Strings (2016) was made in collaboration with Manolo Hernandez (then a student at the Frank Mohr Institute). It turns a spider web into a virtual harp/wind chime (in a similar fashion to some of the models in 1.4), with each string assigned a different note based on length. The gusts of wind create delicately detailed expressive melodies accompanied by the natural sound. This is achieved in real time, with Max/MSP/Jitter watching for movement of trigger points on the strings.

Take Your Seats (2016) was created by assigning the seating positions of the unwitting attendees of the TEDxGroningen event to notes on a virtual fret/chair board. Voicings are created by unconscious social conventions of proximity, and any indecisions create rippling melodies.[32] Mobile phones add higher synth tones. The work was created in just two hours, from the moment when all attendees were seated to the beginning of my presentation – an intense but worthwhile burst of sonification work.

Heart of Mouse (2018) connects data from the heart activity of a mouse to the filters of a large analogue synth. The data includes not just pulse rate but shape (as addressed in Section 2.3). There is something strangely poignant about the small and brief life form generating such a majestic soundscape. Data was provided by Philip Aston (University of Surrey) and Kamalan Jeevaratnam (University of Cambridge).

Doctored Names (2019) converts the Excel file of the University of Surrey 2019 Doctoral College Conference attendees into visualised musical material. Letters are converted to pitches using a custom letter frequency to note frequency system (using an early version of *Crypto* from *DataLoop*). Faculty and discipline provide additional layers including timbral and metric information, the relative sizes of the diverse disciplines creating large-scale formal structures.

---

[32] One indecisive attendee switched seats several times, improvising their own melody.

Public Opinion (2019). In order to track public sentiment responses to news events, here the signing of the petition to revoke Article 50 dictated the tempo of any stored MIDI file, so that every note represents one signature in real time. A virtual performance of *Flight of the Bumblebee*, generated by this process, made the Internet rounds: the lulls and uber-virtuosity reveal the swells of public opinion in response to the then Prime Minister's public announcements.

Tolt (2020) shares an ethos with *Pendulum Music* (and *Arpendulus*) in that it sources rhythmic patterns and arpeggios from the natural world. Here, data from horse gaits are translated to microrhythmic arpeggios. Data from all four limbs – including stance times, 'swing', frequency and relative timings in a number of gaits (Robilliard et al., 2006) – provide rich rhythmic information aligning with previous time-feel models (see Mermikides, 2010:89–99 and 2020a). Each limb can be assigned to the timing and duration of an individual pitch, and collectively create both symmetric and asymmetric patterns that are familiarly equine but beyond my immediate imagination to reproduce. One gait of particular interest is the *tolt* invented (or pioneered) by Icelandic horses, an impressively smooth four-beat lateral pattern existing between the walk and trot.

Head Music (2020). Selen Atasoy and a team of researchers at the University of Oxford have been revealing the harmonic patterns of human brain activity using Fourier analysis (Atasoy et al., 2016). This is analogous to the harmonic analysis of a complex sound or the drawbars of an organ – such that every brain state may be described as a set of amplitudes. These connectome harmonics of brain activity match harmonic wave patterns of certain frequencies and are excited and transformed by changes in brain state, like a complex musical instrument. Atasoy and I worked together to sonify these harmonics, revealing changes in this harmonic profile for a subject – first under placebo and then under the influence of LSD, resulting in a transformation of the upper melodic figuration. Collaborators included Dr Selen Atasoy, Prof Morten Kringelbach (University of Oxford) and Phelan Kane for programming support.

3.1.9 Slow Light (2018–)

Slow Light is a collection of works and associated technologies exploring the translation of visual and colour data to musical parameters. The project title comes from a discussion with Australian classical guitarist and composer Philip Houghton (1954–2017). In our brief and only meeting, we somehow arrived at the topic and agreed that music was nothing more (or less) than slowed-down light – and light, accelerated music for that matter: translocations in the temporal continuum (see Section 2.4). The roots of the project run as early as *Microcosmos* but the principles have now developed into the bespoke

Max4Live sonification instrument *Kandinsky*.[33] This has become central to recent works in colour/light translation, with its ability to automate discrete and continuous colour responses with a variety of layering as well as trajectories through the image beyond the conventional left-right reading. These sonifications can be produced quickly and in real time, and integrated to the mapping, virtual instrument and audio environment of Ableton Live. I have created dozens of pieces and improvisations on classical artworks, video footage, live webcam feeds for exhibitions, presentations and tributes to friends.

Kandinsky works by loading an image or video file and recruiting a digital 'reader' that can examine any selected pixel and report its RGB values – that is, the amount of red, green and blue content, with each represented by a number in the range of 0–255. This colour space can be visualised as a cube with each of its eight corners representing every combination of maximum or minimum values of red, green and blue that is, (255, 255, 255) white, (0, 0, 0) black, (255, 0, 0) red, (255, 255, 0) yellow, (0, 255, 0) green, (0, 255, 255) cyan, (0, 0, 255) blue, and (255, 0, 255) purple. Even with this relatively simple measure, between these corners there exists a cube with a gradient of millions of colours. The reader can be set to move through the image file (or can stay put in one zone of a video file) and report the RGB values continuously or at specified ms or tempo-synced subdivisions. As the reader moves through the two-dimensional image (which can be specified as trajectories within a set tempo-synced duration), it essentially creates a corresponding trajectory through our colour cube. Movements in each of these three colour dimensions can be rapidly mapped to any parameter of a software instrument or process. Zones in colour space can also be used to trigger notes. This process can be thought of as hanging specific pitches in the three-dimensional colour space, which are triggered when a colour comes close to them (how sensitive they are to near-misses, and whether their velocity is affected by this proximity can be controlled). This approach connects us to the historic concept of the colour keyboard (Schedel, 2021), where various diatonic and chromatic notes were connected to specific colours, either through their relative frequencies (with red lowest and violet highest) or through the aesthetic or synaesthetic associations of the composer. These historic colour scales (including those from Newton, Castel and Scriabin) can be called up as presets; but new colour scales can also be created, either manually or by auto-mapping pitches to colours of the current image. Another layer of control is offered through 'colour buses' which allow individual colour notes to be sent only to specific instruments, creating additional layers of bespoke pitch-mappings. Specific colour notes can even be linked to the key and modality of the entire system: a deep red to

---

[33] A previous title, *Synaesthesizer*, was mercifully abandoned.

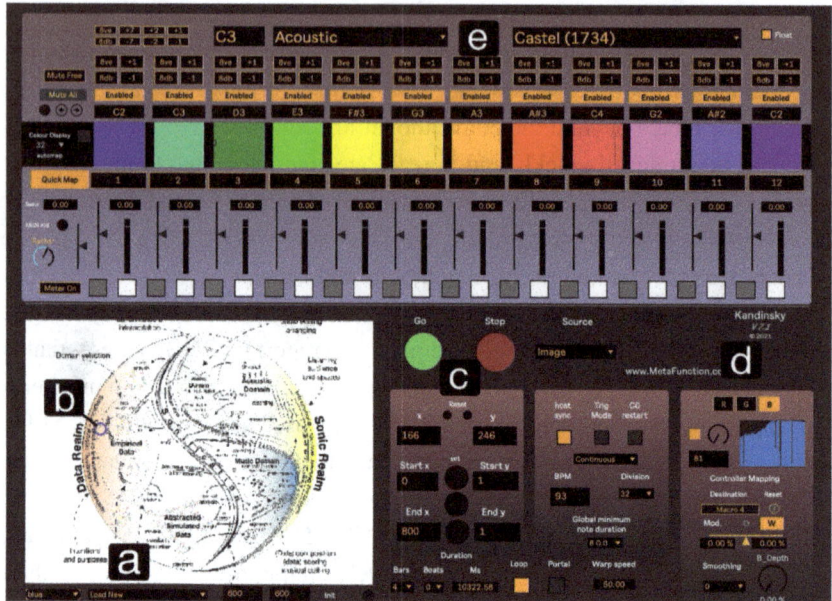

Figure 5 *The Kandinsky interface.* An image or video file is loaded (a), a reader (b), travels in a custom trajectory reporting RGB values at a controllable rate (c). These can be used to map to any parameter (d) or trigger pitches based on historic or custom colour scales (e).

Mixolydian, orange to Dorian and so on. In this way, colours can be assigned to scale degrees, but also alter the underlying mode – a tight metaphor for colouring the canvas. Figure 5 provides a glimpse of the *Kandinsky* interface.

The instrument is also used in more formalised projects, such as Evelyn Glennie's 2018 *Rhythm of Life* radio series where I produced a number of sonifications of prints by Bridget Riley (born 1931) archived at Tate Britain. Of these, a piece derived from a systematic reading of Riley's *Nataraja* (1993) was broadcast. The sonification (translated to notation for violinist Anne-Marie Cundy) captures the complex but satisfying 10:7 tiling dimensions and the almost Shepard-Risset tone sense of constant ascent, occasional breaks and shimmering perceptual confusion.

The inner logic of *Kandinsky* was also employed in *December Hollow* (2020), a collaborative project with the composer, engineer and synthesiser pioneer Peter Zinovieff (1933–2021), and violinist Anne-Marie Cundy. The project is a developed realisation of Zinovieff's (1969) 'fold-out score' concept. The compositional system is designed to generate electronic music and/or conventional scores by slicing through a three-dimensional topographical score (sourced from Zinovieff's geological training) of 'emotional zones'. This implementation of the dormant fifty-year-old vision is documented in the presentation and paper *Revisiting December Hollow* (Mermikides, Zinovieff & Curran-Cundy, 2020).

3.1.10 DataLoop (2019–)

DataLoop is a suite of Max4Live devices distributed to a wide community of electronic musicians through Ableton's educational tours.[34] Developed with programmer and producer Phelan Kane of Metafunction, these devices allow climate data, text, and real-time asteroid and weather data to be translated into MIDI instructions and mapping parameters, directly in the Ableton Live environment. These resources lower the previous Max/MSP 'barrier of entry' through which few musicians pass through (or emerge from), allowing an engagement with stored or real-time data within a familiar DAW environment. *Weather Report* (2019) receives live weather information from global locations including Berlin, Tokyo, London and Pasadena, and their temperature, rainfall, humidity, ozone levels and other values may be mapped to pitch, velocity and controller data. *Asteroid Report* (2019) communicates with the International Space Station to receive real-time data on fifteen asteroids. Information on perihelion distance inclination, eccentricity and several other data streams can be assigned to notes or controller data. *Climate Report* (2019) stores 140 years of NASA-sourced climate data from 1880 to 2020: this can be played through at any tempo, and the various streams of data (CO_2, Ice Mass and Ice Area in Greenland and Antarctica, Temperature Anomaly and Sea Level) can be assigned to any range of pitches or controller data. *Climate Report* was employed in the creation of *Four Warnings for Piano* (2020). Crypto (2019) and Crypto Sequencer (2019) translate letters into pitches, as discussed in the cryptographic systems of Section 2.2. They can do so using the traditional German and French cryptogram systems, or adapted versions which use octave displacement based on capitalisation, convergent mapping or other rules. They can also use a direct ASCII-to-MIDI conversion (as discussed in Section 2.1) or an original system which matches the frequency of a letter in the English language to the frequency of note occurrence in a major or minor key, as derived from a corpus of tonal music (and used in *Doctored Music*). *Crypto* cycles through a string of text from left to right (at any rate or rhythmic pattern), while *Crypto Sequencer* reads through a sixteen-character string laid out in a sixty-four-square grid, through which several trajectories may be initiated.

---

[34] The impetus of the project was a scheduled event at the 2020 Ableton Loop conference in Berlin, cancelled due to the COVID-19 pandemic.

These tools can be employed in quite involved projects, but I also use them quite casually and covertly. They are routinely used in demonstrations, or as creative constraints to spark a piece, or to provide a level of uniqueness to a live performance with the day's weather or venue name imprinted into that one moment, whether revealed to the audience or kept hidden.

3.1.11 Four Warnings for Piano (2020–)

Commissioned by Heidi Leathwood for *The House Explodes: A Concert for the Climate Crisis* (2020). In initial consultation with Rob Scott, a physicist and space scientist, this piece was created through the systematic translation of climate data (CO_2 levels, sea level, temperature and ice mass for 1880 to 2019). No information has been added or removed. Any gaps represent periods where data was not documented or where values are repeated within a fine margin of error. A customised Max for Live device (*Weather Report* from DataLoop) was employed for this project but the statistics are directly sourced from NASA and freely available (see NASA, 2023). The time scale has been compressed to a quaver per year (1880–1958), and one bar per year (a quaver per deciyear) from 1959 on. At the indicated tempo, this results in a performance of approximately two minutes, but any master tempo can be elected. Furthermore, each era (indicated by double barlines) can have its own time scale against that master tempo, so that any musical subdivision can be used to represent a historic time slice. In performance, an analogue metronome placed on the piano clicking at crotchets or quavers can be used to represent the urgent passing of time. This can run for as long as required at the outset of the piece; when we reach our current year, the metronome is stopped, while the piano still resonates. *Four Warnings* may be played by two to four pianists on up to four pianos (with the lines suitably distributed). The ascent of the CO_2, temperature, sea level – and descent of ice mass – are visceral and precipitous, and continue as the data is added incrementally starting from its initial composition.

3.1.12 Genomusicology (2020–)

DNA – with its parallels to cryptographic translation – is tempting fodder for sonification. *Microcosmos* draws on it, as does the piece *ACTG*, which is simply an ASCII translation of all 64 possible codons.[35] *Genomusicology* is

---

[35] A codon is a sequence of three consecutive nucleotides (ACTG). Each codon can send instructions to produce specific proteins, and start and end translations. In *Microcosmos* these were used to create a layer of musical information. In *ACTG* the sixty-four mathematically possible codons (AAA, AAC, AAT etc.) produce trichords where (using ASCII translation) A = 65 (F4), C = 67 (G4), T = 84 (C6) and G = 71 (B4).

a collection of ongoing collaborative projects which extends this DNA sonification so as to meet the 4Rs more fully – particularly the criteria of relevance and recognisability. The 2020 *COVID-19 Listening Project* aimed to communicate the underlying mechanisms of the virus's mutations and strains to a broad audience whose lives at the time were particularly affected by them. It was formed in collaboration with audio researcher and programmer Dr Enzo De Sena (University of Surrey) and in consultation with Gemma Bruno (Telethon Institute of Genetics and Medicine, Italy) and Niki Loverdu (KU Leuven, Belgium). It aimed – through sonification – to reveal and communicate mutation rates and characteristics of the spike protein of the COVID-19 virus and its many evolving strains.

Instead of reading through the DNA sequences and assigning musical material symbolically to codes and their resulting proteins, *COVID-19* uses a comparative analysis of DNA that sounds the *differences* between DNA strands. In this way, one hears mutations in the many strains of the virus, which were fleeting in the population and which persisted. Seven hundred genome sequences from data sets provided by the National Center for Biotechnology Information were processed,[36] and differences in genome pairs were identified using the Needleman–Wunsch global alignment algorithm (Durbin et al.,1998). These mismatches were identified in terms of position in the genome, and the type of mutation (or 'deltas') observed (point mutations, omissions, repetitions, etc.).

The initial process assigned the types of mutation and their position in the genome as – respectively – chromatic notes in metric placement which could later be mapped symbolically to any discrete (or constructed in a continuous) musical objects. This system was employed in the creation of a choral work *Chorus of Changes*. Here, over 500 genome sequences are translated into two octaves of a B-minor scale. The translations are selected by mapping the most common mutation types ('note deltas') into the most common diatonic scale degrees on a sample of Western art music (see Huron, 2008) using the DataLoop *Crypto* device. This results in familiar melodic motifs for the most commonly retained mutations and pandiatonic blurring for the more novel mutations. At the tempo selected, this results in a surprisingly engaging piece of music lasting over forty-two minutes, where the language of mutation is translated into that of motivic transformation, a deeper sonification beyond arbitrary chromatic or 'safe' scale choices. This is performable by choir and organ but is rendered with MIDI instrumentations in Ableton Live with UAD and Native Instrument plugins. The *COVID-19 Listening Project* has been featured on Italian TV's

---

[36] See National Center for Biotechnology Information, 2023.

prime-time current affairs programme *diMartedì*, hosted by Barbara Gallavotti (broadcast on May 19 2020) to about 3 million viewers, and in Metro London on 13 November 2020 (with a circulation of about 1.3 million).

Vax Musicalis employed a similar comparative sonification approach, sounding out the differences between a seasonal flu vaccine and the real-world strains, where the resulting musical motifs were modelled by the virus's resistance to the vaccine. Some strains were whisper quiet, and others had a clear – and unnerving – voice. The *Relative Harmony* project (with collaborators Dr Enzo de Sena, Prof Deborah Dunn-Walters (University of Surrey), Sarah Bailey and Nils Marggraf) turned DNA sonification to the subject of human kinship. Here, we selected various positions ('loci' such as TH01 and VWA) in the human genome commonly used in paternity and maternity tests. Everybody carries two alleles (variations of the DNA in these loci), one inherited from their mother and one from their father (see National Institute of Standards and Technology, 2010). A translation system for these various alleles was set up, using systematic rules to convert each allele into a unique melodic fragment. Each person thus carries a 'melody' made of these two fragments. A child inherits a hybrid melody formed by a fragment from each of its parents (an illustration of the process is presented in Figure 6). There is a compelling beauty (and

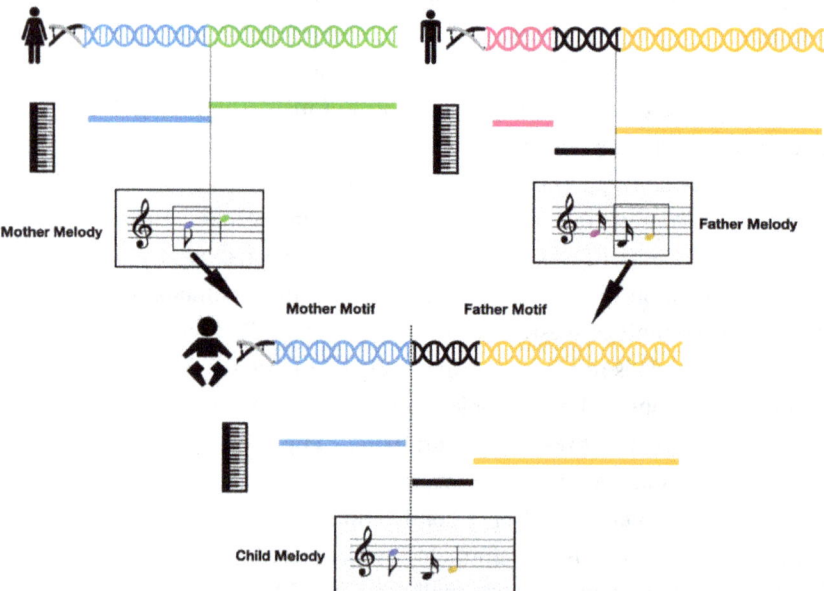

Figure 6 An illustration of the sonification process used in *Relative Harmony*. Inherited alleles encoded as melodic fragments in each parent's melody combine to form a child melody.

metaphorical truth) in the notion that our DNA – and identity – are interweaved melodies of our ancestors, and we can recognise traits of them as motivic. While the sonification examples showed this, I found the extent of the challenge of building a system that identified these distinctions just as meaningful. The distinctions between alleles took significant effort to draw out: rather than our differences, the sonification revealed our universal kinship.

3.2 Unmuddling the Middle: Music and – or as – Sonic Communication

Neuhoff (2019) acknowledges that the 'bifurcation' of 'artistic' and 'empirical' sonification does not mark a clear line but exists on a continuum. However, he suggests that the centrepoint of this continuum is a 'muddled middle' that 'fails to live up to the goals of either art or science' (Neuhoff 2019:329). There is, of course, value in having clear goals, and considering how they are met. There are objective measures of the success of an empirical sonification, such as how accurately and reliably the data is conveyed and to how many subjects. Nonetheless, the goals and measure of success of art are more evasive. We could go by audience feedback, polling listeners on their curiosity, (dis)pleasure, stylistic familiarity, (dis)comfort and outrage. Alternatively, we might delegate the assessment entirely to composers or experts or take a listener–composer balanced score. How do we balance ten infuriated listeners against one who is utterly transfixed? Or the immediate mild pleasure of one listener against the sustained effort of another to contend with the music through repeated listenings? Or an immediate mild pleasure against a disarmed listener who contends with the music beyond the immediate experience? Or a composer who hates her piece against a listener who adores it?

All this is surely of little value: to reduce an evolving multi-dimensional musical experience to a scorecard of failure and success is not only regrettably conservative – failing to acknowledge music's immense potential – it is even profoundly unhistorical, ignoring as it does a long tradition of musical experimentation. Listeners are continuously challenged – and gradually transformed by – such uncompromising sonic material as sustained and insistent repetition, open and infinite forms, geologically slow transformation, frozen moments in time, stylistic disruptions, and sundry unfamiliar objects, be they timbral, microtonal, rhythmic or harmonic. We have long accepted human–machine interaction, mechanistic and generative process, stochastic and indeterminate functions, embrace of the extra-musical and the *meta*, deep exploration of micro-sounds, the borderlands between the pitch and rhythmic domains, statistical density, liminality of perception and idiom, and the beauty of deep dissonance. To imagine music doesn't embrace discomfort, doesn't challenge normative thinking, would be to somehow miss the existence of Russolo, Schaeffer, Cage, Schoenberg, Webern, Stockhausen, Feldman, Varèse, Partch, Xenakis, Ligeti, Lucier, Saariaho, Messiaen, Eno, Penderecki, Reich, Nancarrow, Miles Davis, (John or Alice) Coltrane, (Ornette or Steve) Coleman, Derbyshire, Rampazzi, Radigue, Scriabin, Autechre, Oliveros, Radiohead or the countless others that through past novelty have forged the current foundation of the acceptable.[37]

We should not, of course, be deaf to the differing characteristics of informational listening (gathering information about the world through sound) and familiar music language, and how sonification relates to these. Music routinely operates and relies on the exceptional predictive faculties of the human brain (see, for example, Huron 2008, and the continuing research of the Center for Music in the Brain),[38] employing musical expectancy, multi-level repetition and rhythmic entrainment, among other conditioned responses to auditory stimuli. Even in overtly complex music, our predictive faculties are hacked by significantly limiting various parameters and their latent structures. As a consequence, important structures in conventional music are rather well suited to preservation in the symbol and notation domain. We readily perceive and process striated (gridded) structures in time (see London, 2012), pitch and macro-harmony (Tymoczko, 2011:15). Nor is it an accident that any common pitch-based musical instrument has a particular set of harmonic overtones and variable tones, making possible both auditory segregation (separation from other instruments) and auditory integration (blend among instruments). The stuff of informational listening is quite different. An audification or simple low-level mapping of a typical data source is unlikely to produce such familiar structures as antecedent-consequent phrases, harmonic cadence or binary rhythmic structures. Many instances of data sonification, then, will not call for a normative form of musical listening based on common predictive operation. But not all music relies to the same degree on such structures, and it is possible in our canvas to devise analogic mappings that deploy variously striated templates.[39] Symbolic mappings can even draw on these familiar musical objects, generating and transforming accessible motifs and rhythmic patterns. Music has evolved around our predictive capacities, and sonifiers can opt to engage with this language as little or as much as they wish. If we are using a canvas of diatonic pitch-classes upon which to present the data, then

---

[37] For an introduction to the rich – and long – history of experimentalism see Holmes, 2020.
[38] See https://musicinthebrain.au.dk/.
[39] Note that even though music might typically feature this lattice of pitch, rhythm and timbre, there is ample room for perceptual salience and expressive nuance between – and supported by – these slices (see, for example, Danielsen 2010, Mermikides 2020a and Fabian et al., 2014)

functional harmony or modulation can be used to demarcate subsets of data or temporal periods. If we are presenting a comparative analysis, then an antecedent-consequent phrase structure may be both an accessible and informationally clear choice of sonic display. For example, architectural points of particular physical support may be mapped to corresponding strong and weak beats in a binary temporal structure. Using such techniques allows us – if we wish – to use various objects which 'sound like music' but still meet the 4 R criteria of sonification.

We should also not equate effective musical communication with the superficial characteristics of typical music making such as notation, instruments, intentions and rituals of presentation. Take on the one hand a conventionally composed – but uninspired – MIDI score performed by a virtual string quartet. The 'work' consists of root inversion diatonic triads, played in semibreves, with a fixed dynamic and timbre, and moving in parallel motion. Compare this with the sound of octatonic trails of notes over ominous swells of percussion interweaving searing shards of woodwind trichords, all sourced from volcanic activity and meeting the criteria of hard sonification. Through the simplistic lens of intention and surface appearance the former is music, even if it has no transporting effect, no value to the listener or even the composer. The latter – if not framed as such – would not be music, despite the depth of listener experience.

A related loose end remains, if we accept Scaletti's categorisation of music as a sonification: 'a cross-domain, inference-preserving mapping from thought to sound . . . like mind-melding with the person who created the music.' Then what to make of generative music where the composer has initiated but not pre-heard the music? What of a hard sonification misheard as music? We could discard these moments as artificial experiences: Turing tests of musical automata, simulated but not real musical communication. Simpler – I suggest – to accept that musical patterns may be conceived, and they may be perceived. Almost always these poles of conception and perception are bonded, but that does not preclude or even diminish the enjoyment of 'misheard' music, or musical experiences without a human creator. The 'melding' – even absent another mind – is no less real or profound.

3.3 To the Seas: The Why and Maybe of Sonification

Throughout this Element, it has never been my aim to clutter the discourse on sonification with yet more terms, nor police those in existence. Rather, I have hoped to cast a light on the tangled continua which compose the whole terrain of sonification practice – intentions, translation methods, modes of listening – and to ask how they relate and how they might be symbiotically employed. What remains to discuss is the *why* of sonification. The reported purposes of strictly defined ('hard' or 'empirical') sonification have already been articulated: they include 'conveying information', 'interpreting, understanding, or communicating relations in the domain under study' and 'increasing ... knowledge of the source'. We might collate such purposes under the broad umbrella of *communication*, the delivery of data as non-speech audio so as to enhance knowledge, widen access and modes of learning, and even reveal otherwise hidden properties of the domain under the study. Despite the clarity of these aims, it is less clear to what extent they have been met. Sceptical commentators have asked if sonification is 'doomed to fail' (Neuhoff, 2019) or pointedly ask whether it can boast of any significant successes to date (Supper, 2012). While sonification contains much untapped potential, there seems to be a tendency to ask too much of sonification and dismiss anything that falls short. For some critics, a sonification is only successful if it presents all the data accurately, with little context or explanation, while at the same time sounding like the narrow range of music that the critic happens to like. It's like asking for a visual graph to be useful out of context, for it to simultaneously operate without axes, present the data and look like the work of a narrow range of familiar artists. To be sure, it may be possible to get close to all or some of these aims, but when it is not, we should embrace the abundance of humble but fruitful opportunities. As part of the 'cascade' (Scaletti, 2021:377) of materials used to impart knowledge (text, tables, figures, graphs, animations, etc.), sonification is a readily employable resource. We live in an increasingly sonified world, thinking nothing of sonic symbols of connecting, disconnecting and pairing Bluetooth devices, messages sent and received, device status switches, exhausted and replenished batteries, auto shut-offs of devices, and more – all without training. With some listener guidance, sonification can be harnessed to augment the learning of more complex concepts. I have produced sonic pedagogical resources for undergraduate material in biology, statistics and physics, and despite their novelty, they are as basic – and as useful – as these other objects of knowledge, enabling a multi-modal engagement with material. Many of these instructive sonifications make abstract knowledge concrete and memorable; often, in fact, they activate the predictive mechanisms shared by conventional musical communication to deliver – for me, at least – a memorable musical experience.

The practice of data music (or a more openly defined sonification) offers additional potential benefits. In addition to **C1 – Communication** I suggest three more broad categories: **C2 – Catharsis/Connection/Celebration, C3 – Compositional insight/Creative constraint** and

C4 – **Collaboration/Common language**. These I present collectively as the **4Cs** to complement the **4Rs** of Hermann's sonification criteria (see Section 1.5).[40] Here is an overview:

C1) A visceral **communication** of data. When it comes to gaining data about the world, we take graphs and tables for granted, and yet the sonic domain is no more arbitrary or abstracted a medium, and in some contexts it is more sophisticated. For example, sound, unlike a flat image, is temporally bounded and necessarily unfolding in time, and we as humans have developed sophisticated auditory predictive systems that may be readily exploited. The late flourishes in the systematic translation of climate change (*Four Warnings for Piano*) are genuinely alerting in the most primal sense. The real-time realisation of population growth in *Birth/Death* (deaths in the left hand of the piano, births in the right) engage in a way that the reported numbers do not, as does the spread and genomic evolution or progression of disease (*Outbreak, Chorus of Changes*).

C2) **Catharsis** and emphatic engagement from the 'sounding out' of otherwise hidden inner experience (e.g. blood cell activity during leukaemia treatment (*Bloodlines*), the phasing and disrupted rhythms of insomnia (*Sound Asleep*) and the stressful schedule of nurses' work hours. Music's ability not just to present data but to make it felt invites an empathic turn 'when I and you becomes I am you, or I might you' (Spiro et al in Mermikides, A., 2021:141). In this category we might also include a sense of **connection** to – and **celebration** of events, processes, humans and other animals – from the apparently important to the apparently mundane. Instead of being lost, these things are captured, voiced and shared.

C3) **Compositional insight**. Sonification provides an endless source of novel **compositional** techniques and **creative constraints**, both of which quiet the 'judging spectre' of the creative process. I find sonification provides a meaningful constraint that inhibits compositional habits and transforms the blank canvas from problem to puzzle, with some sort of rewarding solution always available. The techniques and concepts acquired in the process are transportable to conventional compositional practice (for example in *Tolt, Transitions* and *Arpendulus*). More fundamentally, an act of sonification can inspire – and give meaning to – a piece that would not otherwise exist, regardless of its adherence to various criteria.

---

[40] Only the most attentive readers might note the parallel here of the Rs and Cs to Team R and Team C in the *Where the Wind Blows* piece of Section 1.4.

C4) **Collaboration.** Sonification stimulates the creation of genuinely **collaborative** networks that dissolve the traditional delineations of scientist and artist, along with concomitant notions of exclusive creativity and knowledge, in favour of a **common** conceptual and aesthetic language.

Sonification – from the referencing of extra-musical material to full engagement with Hermann's rules – is open to engagement by all composers, as compositional impetus, creative constraint and the seductive challenge of the aesthetic transformation of data communication. In coming to terms with the 4Rs and questioning the transparency – and effective communication – of the translation system, we advance knowledge of both the domain under study and music itself. The composer needs only to connect with the data and its underlying mechanisms and to consider how best to communicate them in sound. There is no need for anyone to occupy a static position on the empirical-artistic devising continuum. I see no reason why, for example, a piece of 'pure' sonification cannot be used as a single movement (or section or component) within a conventionally composed work, or why the composer may not move from project to project with the same techniques but different communicative goals. What remains central to the composer is the challenge of effective sonic communication, be it musical ideas, expressive content or the choreography of the natural world.

Scientific inquiry aims to tease out – from the noise of disorder – meaningful patterns, illuminating nature's mechanics and making sense of the world. Similarly, music composition forges low-entropy structures amidst the noise of waves in the audio or acoustic domains. These structures may be entirely missed by the unmusical or inattentive listener or deeply impactful to another. Be they melodic, harmonic or timbral, they can be transmitted and transformed, yet still remain recognisable through the various boundaries of conception, sounding out and listening. The rewards of discovering order and structure (however simple or complex) amid the background of chaos are enjoyed by science and music alike, so that their mapping and integration seems natural.

In both the data and sonic realms, patterns of information are not abstract but physical imprints, be they in the earth and stars, cables and drives, brains and bodies, water or air. Like footprints in the sand, these patterns may be fleeting. But we can choose to take a moment to explore, admire and share them with each other, before they are washed back to the sea of entropy.

References

Aksenov, A. N. (1973). Tuvin folk music. *Asian Music*, 4(2): 7–18.

Anderson, J. (1997). Notes to Murail's *Mémoires/Erosion*. CD Accord.

Atasoy, S., Donnelly, I. & Pearson, J. (2016). Human brain networks function in connectome-specific harmonic waves. *Nature Communications* 7: 10340. DOI: https://doi.org/10.1038/ncomms10340.

Barrass, S. & Vickers, P. (2011). Sonification design and aesthetics, in Hermann, T., Hunt, A. & Neuhoff, J. G., eds. *The Sonification Handbook*: 145–171. Logos Publishing House.

Bastan, D. (2022). *Inspired by Nature.* Ableton Live Pack, www.ableton.com/en/packs/inspired-nature/.

Baxter, I. (2020). *Sonification as a means to generative music*, PhD thesis, University of Sheffield. https://etheses.whiterose.ac.uk/27591/.

BBC (2015). *Radio 4 Midweek.* 28 October. www.bbc.co.uk/programmes/b06kdrfd.

Brazil, E. & Fernström, M. (2011). Auditory icons, in Hermann, T., Hunt, A. & Neuhoff, J. G., eds. *The Sonification Handbook*: 325–335. Logos Publishing House.

Buckle, B. (2022). *Spectrogram art: A short history of musicians hiding visuals inside their tracks*, https://mixmag.net/feature/spectrogram-art-music-aphex-twin.

Code, D. L. (2023). Can musical encryption be both? A survey of music-based ciphers. *Cryptologia*, 47(4): 318–364, DOI: https://doi.org/10.1080/01611194.2021.2021565.

Danielsen, A. (Ed.). (2010). *Musical Rhythm in the Age of Digital Reproduction* (1st ed.). Routledge.

Dombois, F. & Eckel G. (2011). Audification, in Hermann, T., Hunt, A., & Neuhoff, J. G., eds. *The Sonification Handbook*: 301–320. Logos Publishing House.

Durbin, R., Eddy, S., Krogh, A. & Mitchison, G. (1998). *Biological Sequence Analysis*. Cambridge University Press.

Enyart, J. W. (1984). The symphonies of Heitor Villa-Lobos. PhD dissertation. University of Cincinnati.

Fabian, D., Timmers, R. & Schubert, E. (Eds.). (2014). *Expressiveness in Music Performance: Empirical Approaches across Styles and Cultures* (1st ed.). Oxford University Press.

Gleick, J. (2011). *The Information: A History, a Theory, a Flood*. Fourth Estate.

References

Glennie, E. (2018). *The Rhythm of Life*. BBC Radio 4. www.bbc.co.uk/programmes/b0bgfqx7.

Gresham-Lancaster, S. (2012). Relationships of sonification to music and sound art. *AI & Society*, 27(2): 207–212.

Grond, F. & Berger, J. (2011). Parameter mapping sonification, in Hermann, T., Hunt, A., & Neuhoff, J. G., eds., *The Sonification Handbook*, chapter 15: 363–397. Logos Publishing House.

Hermann, T. (2010). *Sonification: A Definition*. http://sonification.de/son/definition.

Hermann, T. (2023). *Sonification.de*. [Website.] http://sonification.de.

Hermann, T., Hunt, A. & Neuhoff, J. G., eds. (2011). *The Sonification Handbook*. Logos Publishing House.

Hey Exit (2015). *Every Recording of Gymnopédie 1*. https://soundcloud.com/hey-exit/every-recording-of-gymnopedie-1.

Holmes, T. (2020). *Electronic and Experimental Music: Technology, Music, and Culture* (6th ed.). Routledge.

Huron, D. (2008). *Sweet Anticipation: Music and the Psychology of Expectation*. Massachusetts Institute of Technology Press.

Huss, M. (2024) 'Unforgotten grooves: Reading and Listening to Rainer Maria Rilke's *Primal Sound*' in Groth S. K. & Frisk, H., eds (2024) *Traces of Sound: Reflections of Sounds Unheard* (2024): 37–50. Lund: The Sound Environment Centre at Lund University.

ITU (2009). International Morse Code Recommendation. Radiocommunication Sector. Itu.int (Report). ITU Recommendation. International Telecommunication Union. October. ITU-R M.1677-1.

Juslin, P. N. (2013). From everyday emotions to aesthetic emotions: Towards a unified theory of musical emotions. *Physics of Life Reviews*, 10(3): 235–266.

Kahneman, D. (2011). *Thinking, Fast and Slow*. Farrar, Straus and Giroux.

Kepler, J., Aiton, E. J., Duncan, A. M. & Field, J. V. (1997). *The Harmony of the World*. American Philosophical Society.

Kramer, G. (1994). An introduction to auditory display. In G. Kramer (Ed.), *Auditory display: Sonification, audification, and auditory interfaces* (pp. 1–78). Reading, MA: Addison Wesley.

Kramer, G., Walker, B., Bonebright, T., Cook, P., Flowers J. H., Miner, N. & Neuhoff, J. (1999). Sonification report: Status of the field and research agenda prepared for the National Science Foundation by Members of the International Community for Auditory Display [White paper]. http://sonify.psych.gatech.edu/publications/pdfs/1999-NSF-Report.pdf.

Langton, J. (2020). Systems, objects and space in the work of Beatriz Ferreyra, Delia Derbyshire, Éliane Radigue and Teresa Rampazzi. PhD Thesis. University of Surrey.

Lehman, F. (2013). Transformational analysis and the representation of genius in film music. *Music Theory Spectrum*, 35(1): 1–22.

Lewand, R. (2000). *Cryptological Mathematics*. Mathematical Association of America.

London, J. (2012). *Hearing in Time: Psychological Aspects of Musical Meter* (2nd ed). Oxford University Press.

Mayo, N. (1997). Ocean waves: Their energy and power', *Physics Teacher*, 35: 352–356.

Mermikides, M. (2010). Changes over time: Theory & practice. PhD Thesis. University of Surrey.

Mermikides, M. (2020a). 'Straight and Late': Analytical perspectives on Coltrane's time-feel, *Jazz Perspectives*, 12(1): 147–166.

Mermikides, M. (2020b). *Two Blue Circles for Classical Guitar and Electronics*. Viribus.

Mermikides, A. (2021). *Performance, Medicine and the Human*. London: Methuen Drama.

Mermikides, M. (2022a). Diamonds, abaci, and hexagrams: Exploring the pitch surface of the guitar fretboard. *Soundboard Scholar*, vol. 8. https://digital commons.du.edu/sbs/vol8/iss1/17/.

Mermikides, M. (2022b). *The Modal Compass: 3 Ways to Navigate the Modes*. https://youtu.be/eMHRCfeozVo.

Mermikides, M. & Feygelson, E. (2017). The shape of musical improvisation, in Leech-Wilkinson, D. l. & Prior, H. M., eds., *Music and Shape*, vol. 1: 170–204. Oxford University Press.

Mermikides, M., Zinovieff, P. & Curran-Cundy, A. (2020). Revisiting December Hollow: Unearthing emotive shape, in Weinel, J., Bowen, J. P., Diprose, G. & Lamport N., eds., Proceedings of EVA London 2020 (EVA 2020), BCS. DOI: https://doi.org//10.14236/ewic/EVA2020.16.

Millar, J. & Cage, J. (2010). *Every Day Is a Good Day: The Visual Art of John Cage*. Hayward Publishing.

Mitchell, J. (1994). *Joni Mitchell: The Magdalene Laundries (Live Toronto 1994)*. www.youtube.com/watch?v=ATaFyIbd5hY.

NASA (2023). *Earthdata: Open Access for Open Science*. www.earthdata.nasa.gov/.

National Center for Biotechnology Information (2023). *SARS-CoV-2 Data Hub*. www.ncbi.nlm.nih.gov/sars-cov-2/.

National Institute of Standards and Technology (2010). STR Fact Sheet. https://strbase.nist.gov/str_VWA.htm.

Neuhoff, J. G. (2019). Is sonification doomed to fail? *Proceedings of the 25th International Conference on Auditory Display* (ICAD). DOI: https://doi.org/10.21785/icad2019.069.

New Scientist (2021). Escape Pod: #3 Music: The jazz swing of birdsong and the sonification of the orbits of planets. https://podbay.fm/p/new-scientist-escape-pod/e/1612281600.

Palmer, A. (2023). *Angela Palmer: Gallery*. www.angelaspalmer.com/gallery.

Potter, G. D. M., Skene, D. J., Arendt, J., Cade, J. E., Grant, P. J. & Hardie, L. J. (2016). Circadian rhythm and sleep disruption: Causes, metabolic consequences, and countermeasures. *Endocrine Reviews*, 37(6): 584–608.

Rilke, R. M. (1919), 'Ur-Geräusch', Das Inselschiff: Eine zweitmonatsschrift 1(1), 14–20.

Robilliard, J. J., Thilo., P. & Wilson, A. M. (2006). Gait characterisation and classification in horses. *Journal of Experimental Biology*, 210(2): 187–197.

Sams, E. (1980). Cryptography, musical, in Sadie, S. (ed.), *The New Grove Dictionary of Music and Musicians*. DOI: https://doi.org/10.1093/gmo/9781561592630.article.06915.

Sapir, E. (2014) Language: an introduction to the study of speech. Cambridge: Cambridge University Press.

Sawe, N., & Chafe, C. & Treviño, J. (2020). Using data sonification to overcome science literacy, numeracy, and visualization barriers in science communication. *Frontiers in Communication*, 5. DOI: htttps://doi.org/10.3389/fcomm.2020.00046.

Scaletti, C. (2021). Sonification ≠ Music, in McLean, A. and Dean, R. T. (2021) *The Oxford Handbook of Algorithmic Music*. New York: Oxford University Press: 376–385.

Schedel, M. (2021). Color is the keyboard: Transcoding from visual to sonic, in McLean, A. and Dean, R. T. (2021) *The Oxford Handbook of Algorithmic Music*. New York: Oxford University Press: 387–422.

Scholz, D. S., Rohde, S., Nikmaram, N., Brückner, H. P., Großbach, M., Rollnik, J. D., & Altenmüller, E. O. (2016). Sonification of arm movements in stroke rehabilitation: A novel approach in neurologic music therapy. *Frontiers in Neurology*, 7: 106.

Shannon, C. E. (1948). A mathematical theory of communication. *Bell System Technical Journal*, 27: 379–423, 623–656.

Slonimsky, N. (1945). *Music in Latin America*. New York: Thomas Y. Crowell.

Sorensen, N. (2010). *Harvard Natural Sciences Lecture Demonstration: Pendulum Waves.* https://www.youtube.com/watch?v=yVkdfJ9PkRQ.

Stark, E. A., Vuust, P. and Kringelbach, M. L. (2018). Music, dance, and other art forms: New insights into the links between hedonia (pleasure) and eudaimonia (well-being), in *Progress in Brain Research.* Elsevier: 129–152.

Stevner, A. B. A., Vidaurre, D., Cabral, J., Rapuano, K., Nielsen, S. F. V., Tagliazucchi, E., Laufs, H., Vuust, P., Deco, G., Woolrich, M. W., Van Someren, E., & Kringelbach, M. L. (2019). Discovery of key whole-brain transitions and dynamics during human wakefulness and non-REM sleep. *Nature Communications,* 10(1): 1035.

Supper, A. (2012). The Search for the 'killer application': Drawing the boundaries around the sonification of scientific data. In T. Pinch & K. Bijstervel eds., *The Oxford Handbook of Sound Studies.* Oxford University Press: 249–270.

Supper, A. (2016). Lobbying for the ear, listening with the whole body: The (anti-)visual culture of sonification, *Sound Studies,* 2(1): 69–80.

Tanczos, A. (2014). Villa-Lobos's New York Skyline Melody Visualisation. https://www.youtube.com/watch?v=TiF80x7KfC8

Tufte, E. R. (2001). *The Visual Display of Quantitative Information.* 2nd ed. Cheshire, CT: Graphics Press.

Tymoczko, D. (2011). *A Geometry of Music: Harmony and Counterpoint in the Extended Common Practice.* Oxford University Press.

Vickers, P. (2016). Sonification and music, music and sonification, in *The Routledge Companion to Sounding Art.* Routledge, London: 135–144.

Wishart, T., & Emmerson, S. (1996). *On Sonic Art.* Harwood Academic Publishers.

Worrall, D. (2009). *Sonification and Information: Concepts, instruments and techniques.* University of Canberra.

Worrall, D. (2011). An introduction to data sonification, in Dean, R. T., ed., *The Oxford Handbook of Computer Music.* Oxford: Oxford University Press: 312–333.

Zinovieff, P. (1969). The special case of inspiration computer music scores. *London Magazine,* 100: 165–176.

Acknowledgements

I am indebted to Bridget, Chloe and my late, great mentors Michael Mermikides, Pat Martino and Peter Zinovieff. Deepest thanks to my wonderful family, the NHS, past and present students, colleagues and collaborators (critically Professor Morten Kringelbach, Professor Debra Skene, the Ableton family, Phelan Kane and Anna Tanczos and the late Simon Park). Further thanks for valuable feedback go to Jonathan Leathwood, George Hrab, John McGrath, Olga Mermikides (also for my life), and Alex Mermikides (also for my second life).

Dedication

For Plaka Asini

This publication would not be possible without the enduring influence of my family: my late father, Dr Michael Mermikides (1940–1991), a nuclear physicist who spoke of science, music and humour in the same breath; my wife, Bridget – the best guitarist and musician in the house; and my daughter, Chloe, whose unlikely existence gives meaning to it all. I also owe an incalculable debt to my family of various genetic relations, and the students, colleagues and collaborators from whom I have learnt so much and feel permission to do this. However, in the spirit of this Element's drift from musical anthropocentrism, I choose to dedicate it to a non-human influence.

I write this while overlooking the Argolikos Kolpos, a glistening and isolated gulf in the Greek Peloponnese. This smattering of islands, naturally evolved but perfectly proportioned beach, twinkling seas and impossible skies has been the unchanging backdrop to decades of summers and remains a refuge of renewal and creative inspiration. The region's intersection of astronomical, meteorological and oceanographic cycles, accompanied by a rich sound canvas of cicada white noise, metronomic hoots of the *Sciops* owl, pianissimo interludes and water-wind cross-rhythms has been my constant backdrop to guitar practice, composition, theoretical musings and the perhaps inevitable merging of nature, sound and music.

And so it is to this Plaka Asini region I dedicate this Element. And for those requiring specificity, we will define it as a diamond region with vertices at (1) the horizon-hugging Πλατια island, (2) the ancient and stoic acropolis of Asini, (3) the lone church-and-tree-topped mountain of Λοφος του Προφητη Ηλια in Agia Paraskevi and (4) Kyria Sofia's *Φουρνος* – an irresistible bakery in the neighbouring village of Drepanon.

Cambridge Elements

Twenty-First Century Music Practice

Simon Zagorski-Thomas
London College of Music, University of West London

Simon Zagorski-Thomas is a Professor at the London College of Music (University of West London, UK) and founded and runs the 21st Century Music Practice Research Network. He is series editor for the Cambridge Elements series and Bloomsbury book series on 21st Century Music Practice. He is ex-chairman and co-founder of the Association for the Study of the Art of Record Production. He is a composer, sound engineer and producer and is, currently, writing a monograph on practical musicology. His books include *Musicology of Record Production* (2014; winner of the 2015 IASPM Book Prize), *The Art of Record Production: an Introductory Reader for a New Academic Field* co-edited with Simon Frith (2012), the *Bloomsbury Handbook of Music Production* co-edited with Andrew Bourbon (2020) and the *Art of Record Production: Creative Practice in the Studio* co-edited with Katia Isakoff, Serge Lacasse and Sophie Stévance (2020).

About the Series

Elements in Twenty-First Century Music Practice has developed out of the 21st Century Music Practice Research Network, which currently has around 250 members in 30 countries and is dedicated to the study of what Christopher Small termed musicking – the process of making and sharing music rather than the output itself. Obviously this exists at the intersection of ethnomusicology, performance studies, and practice pedagogy / practice-led-research in composition, performance, recording, production, musical theatre, music for screen and other forms of multi-media musicking. The generic nature of the term '21st Century Music Practice' reflects the aim of the series to bring together all forms of music into a larger discussion of current practice and to provide a platform for research about any musical tradition or style. It embraces everything from hip-hop to historically informed performance and K-pop to Inuk throat singing.

Cambridge Elements

Twenty-First Century Music Practice

Elements in the Series

The Marks of a Maestro: Annotating Mozart's 'Jupiter' Symphony
Raymond Holden and Stephen Mould

Chinese Street Music: Complicating Musical Community
Samuel Horlor

Reimagine to Revitalise: New Approaches to Performance Practices Across Cultures
Charulatha Mani

A Philosophy of Playing Drum Kit: Magical Nexus
Gareth Dylan Smith

Shared Listenings: Methods for Transcultural Musicianship and Research
Stefan Östersjö, Nguyễn Thanh Thủy, David G. Hebert and Henrik Frisk

Repetition and Performance in the Recording Studio
Rod Davies

Original Pirate Material: The Streets and Hip-Hop Transatlantic Exchange
Justin A. Williams

Hidden Music: The Composer's Guide to Sonification
Milton Mermikides

A full series listing is available at: www.cambridge.org/emup

For EU product safety concerns, contact us at Calle de José Abascal, 56–1°, 28003 Madrid, Spain or eugpsr@cambridge.org.

www.ingramcontent.com/pod-product-compliance
Lightning Source LLC
LaVergne TN
LVHW020333260326
834688LV00037B/1005